ABNORMAL PSYCHOLOGY

Longman Essential Psychology
Series editor: Andrew M. Colman

ABNORMAL PSYCHOLOGY

EDITED BY

Arnold A. Lazarus
and
Andrew M. Colman

LONGMAN
London and New York

Longman Group Limited
Longman House, Burnt Mill
Harlow, Essex CM20 2JE, England
and Associated Companies throughout the world.

*Published in the United States of America
by Longman Publishing, New York*

© 1994 Routledge
This edition © 1995 Longman Group Limited
Compilation © 1995 Andrew Colman

This edition first published 1995

ISBN 0 582 27807 4 PPR

British Library Cataloguing-in-Publication Data
A catalogue record for this book is available from the British Library.

Library of Congress Cataloging-in-Publication Data
A catalogue record for this book is available from the Library of Congress.

Typeset by 25 in 10/12pt Times
Printed and bound by Bookcraft (Bath) Ltd

CONTENTS

NOTES ON EDITORS AND CONTRIBUTORS

SIMON BARON-COHEN studied human sciences at New College, Oxford, followed by a doctorate in experimental psychology at University College London. He has taught at University College London and the Institute of Psychiatry, London, where he is currently Senior Lecturer in Developmental Psychology. He is co-editor (with H. Tager-Flusberg and D. J. Cohen) of *Understanding Other Minds: Perspectives from Autism* (1993), and co-author (with P. Bolton) of *Autism: the facts* (1993).

CONNIE CAHILL studied psychology and philosophy at University College, Dublin. She is now a member of the Cognitive Neuropsychiatry Project at the Medical Research Council Cyclotron Unit and University College London. Her clinical experience and research interests lie chiefly within the domains of mental illness, in particular schizophrenia, and neuropsychology.

ANDREW M. COLMAN is Reader in Psychology at the University of Leicester, having previously taught at Rhodes and Cape Town Universities in South Africa. He is the founder and former editor of the journal *Current Psychology* and Chief Examiner for the British Psychological Society's Qualifying Examination. His books include *Facts, Fallacies and Frauds in Psychology* (1987), *What is Psychology? The Inside Story* (2nd edn, 1988), and *Game Theory and its Applications in the Social and Biological Sciences* (2nd edn, 1995).

PETER J. COOPER is the Lecturer in Psychopathology in the Departments of Psychiatry and Experimental Psychology at the University of Cambridge. He conducted his doctoral research and received clinical training in the Department of Psychiatry of the University of Oxford. His research has principally concerned psychiatric aspects of obstetrics and gynaecology, and eating disorders. He has published in psychiatry and psychology journals on the nature, epidemiology, assessment, and treatment of eating disorders. His books include *Bulimia Nervosa: A Guide to Recovery* (1993) and (co-editededit with A. Stein) *Feeding Problems and Eating Disorders in Children and Adolescents* (1992).

vi

CHRIS FRITH studied psychology at Cambridge and the Institute of Psychiatry in London. From 1975 to 1990 he worked on the neuropsychology of schizophrenia with Tim Crow's group at the Clinical Research Centre, Northwick Park Hospital, London. Currently he is working on functional brain imaging at the Medical Research Council Cyclotron Unit and holds an MRC grant at the Psychology Department of University College London, where he is Visiting Professor. He is author of *The Cognitive Neuropsychology of Schizophrenia* (1992).

ISABEL R. HARGREAVES received her PhD at the Department of Psychology, University College of North Wales, Bangor. She has been working as a Clinical Psychologist in Adult Mental Health in Gwynedd since 1984 and is also the Deputy Director of the North Wales Clinical Psychology Course. Her main clinical interests are cognitions and how they affect emotional states.

ARNOLD A. LAZARUS holds the rank of Distinguished Professor of Psychology at Rutgers University, New Brunswick, New Jersey, where he serves on the faculty of the Graduate School of Applied and Professional Psychology. Previously he was a faculty member of Stanford Universty, Temple University Medical School, and Yale University, where he served as Director of Clinical training before moving to Rutgers University in 1972. He has received many awards and honours, most recently the Distinguished Psychologist Award from the Psychotherapy Division of the American Psychological Association. He has published over 200 articles and book chapters and fifteen books including *The Essential Arnold Lazarus* (edited by W. Dryden, 1991), and he is the innovator of an assessment and treatment approach called 'Multimodal Therapy'.

GEOFFREY LOWE is Senior Lecturer in Psychology at the University of Hull. He was previously at the University of Nottingham and Visiting Professor at the University of Tennessee. He is an assistant editor of *The Psychologist*. He has published articles on alcohol and related drugs in *Psychopharmacology*, *British Journal of Addiction*, and *Addiction Research*, and has recently completed a book on *Adolescent Drinking and Family Life*.

J. MARK G. WILLIAMS is Professor of Clinical Psychology at the University College of North Wales, Bangor, having been Research Scientist at the Medical Research Council's Applied Psychology Unit in Cambridge. He is also an Anglican priest, and interested in the interface of psychology with religion. He is co-author (with F. N. Watts, C. MacLeod, and A. Mathews) of *Cognitive Psychology and Emotional Disorders* (1988) and author of *The Psychological Treatment of Depression: A Guide to the Theory and Practice of Cognitive Behaviour Therapy* (2nd edn, 1992).

SERIES EDITOR'S PREFACE

The *Longman Essential Psychology* series comprises twelve concise and inexpensive paperback volumes covering all of the major topics studied in undergraduate psychology degree courses. The series is intended chiefly for students of psychology and other subjects with psychology components, including medicine, nursing, sociology, social work, and education. Each volume contains five or six accessibly written chapters by acknowledged authorities in their fields, and each chapter includes a list of references and a small number of recommendations for further reading.

Most of the material was prepared originally for the Routledge *Companion Encyclopedia of Psychology* but with a view to later paperback subdivision – the contributors were asked to keep future textbook readers at the front of their minds. Additional material has been added for the paperback series: new co-editors have been recruited for nine of the volumes that deal with highly specialized topics, and each volume has a new introduction, a glossary of technical terms including a number of entries written specially for this edition, and a comprehensive new index.

I am grateful to my literary agents Sheila Watson and Amanda Little for clearing a path through difficult terrain towards the publication of this series, to Sarah Caro of Longman for her patient and efficient preparation of the series, to Brian Parkinson, David Stretch, and Susan Dye for useful advice and comments, and to Carolyn Preston for helping with the compilation of the glossaries.

ANDREW M. COLMAN

INTRODUCTION

Arnold A. Lazarus
Rutgers University, New Jersey, USA

Andrew M. Colman
University of Leicester, England

Abnormal psychology is devoted to the study of mental, emotional, and behavioural aberrations. It is the branch of psychology, concerned with research into the classification, causation, diagnosis, prevention, and treatment of psychological disorders or psychopathology. Its purview covers a broad spectrum of afflictions and includes neuroses, psychoses, personality disorders, psychophysiological disorders, organic mental syndromes, and mental retardation. Abnormal psychology is not synonymous with clinical psychology, which is mainly concerned with professional practice and focuses primarily on diagnostic tests and the application of different treatment approaches. The essence of abnormal psychology is its emphasis on research into abnormal behaviour and its endeavour to classify the wide range of mental and emotional aberrations into coherent categories and to understand them. Abnormal psychology serves as a backdrop or guide to clinical practice.

What is abnormal behaviour? It is indeed a challenge to provide a widely accepted definition, but most authorities seem to agree on the following key components. First, statistically, abnormal behaviour tends to be infrequent in the general population (for example, not too many people suffer from hallucinations or are subject to incapacitating depression). A second component is that abnormal behaviour often disregards social norms. Every society has implicit and explicit rules of conduct. Those who violate these regulations may be seen as abnormal in certain respects – although what is abnormal in one culture may be the norm in another. Third, the notion of personal suffering is another important component. Personal distress, for instance, is seen in people suffering from anxiety disorders and depression. The fourth component relates to some disability because of which the individual is unable to pursue a desired goal. Thus, substance abuse creates occupational or social disability (for example, poor work performance or arguments with family members) and can lead to widespread dysfunctions. Finally, abnormal behaviour is often exaggerated. Everyone is subject to certain worries, fears, insecurities, feelings of depression, and so forth, but these feelings become abnormal only when their intensity is unexpectedly severe. Thus, someone who is financially well off but worries continually about money matters is exhibiting an exaggerated form of behaviour. The changing nature of the field of abnormal psychology makes it impossible to offer a simple definition that completely captures its essential features. The combination of the foregoing five components constitutes a partial definition that is not equally applicable to every diagnosis.

The American Psychiatric Association publishes a *Diagnostic and Statistical Manual of Mental Disorders*, which is now in its fourth revised edition (1994), known as *DSM–IV*. This 880-page tome incorporates the most detailed classification of mental disorders. Its diagnostic criteria serve as useful general guidelines and are widely used by researchers and mental health practitioners, especially psychologists and psychiatrists. The *DSM* lists seventeen categories or types of mental disorder including disorders usually first diagnosed in infancy, childhood, or adolescence; mental disorders due to a general medical condition; schizophrenia and other psychotic disorders; mood disorders; anxiety disorders; eating disorders; sleep disorders; adjustment disorders; and personality disorders.

An important and distinctive feature of the *DSM* is its multiaxial system that facilitates treatment planning and outcome predictions. There are five axes in the *DSM–IV* classification:

Axis I: Clinical disorders. Other conditions that may be a focus of clinical attention.
Axis II: Personality disorders. Mental retardation.
Axis III: General medical conditions.
Axis IV: Psychosocial and environmental problems.
Axis V: Global assessment of functioning.

Note that the term "neuroses" does not appear in this system. Axis I includes mood disorders, anxiety disorders, schizophrenia and other psychotic disorders, disorders usually first diagnosed in childhood (of which infantile autism is a prime example), eating disorders, and substance-related disorders (alcohol and drug addiction). Each of the foregoing is the subject of one of the chapters in this book. This volume therefore concentrates specifically on six major groups of clinical disorders. (Other Axis I or Clinical Disorders include adjustment disorders, somatoform disorders, factitious disorders, dissociative disorders, sexual and gender identity disorders, sleep disorders, impulse-control disorders, as well as delirium, dementia, amnestic and other cognitive disorders.)

Although the present volume does not address any Axis II disorders, the reader may be interested in knowing the list of personality disorders included in *DSM–IV*. They are: paranoid personality disorder (a pattern of suspiciousness and distrust wherein others' motives are interpreted as malevolent); schizoid personality disorder (a pattern of detachment from social relationships and a restricted range of emotional expression); schizotypal personality disorder (a pattern of intense discomfort in close relationships, eccentric behaviour, and perceptual or cognitive distortions); antisocial personality disorder (a pattern of disregard for, and violation of, other people's rights); borderline personality disorder (a pattern of unstable relationships, poor or fluctuating self-image, marked impulsiveness, and emotional hypersensitivity); histrionic personality disorder (a pattern of extreme emotionality and attention seeking); narcissistic personality disorder (a pattern of grandiosity, need for admiration, and lack of empathy); avoidant personality disorder (a pattern of social inhibition, feelings of inadequacy, and hypersensitivity to criticism); dependent personality disorder (a pattern of submissive and clinging behaviour tied into an excessive need to be taken care of); obsessive-compulsive personality disorder (a pattern of preoccupation with orderliness, perfectionism, and control); and personality disorder not otherwise specified (a category that provides for people who may have the traits of several personality disorders without meeting the criteria for any specific one, or for those who have a disorder not included in the basic classification, such as a passive-aggressive personality disorder). In essence, the diagnosis of a personality disorder calls for personality traits that are inflexible, enduring, widespread, maladaptive, and cause significant functional impairment or subjective distress. There are many abnormal psychology texts that cover the entire range of *DSM–IV* categories, but the one that we find especially comprehensive and engaging is the book by Davison and Neale (1994).

Turning now to the contents of the present volume, chapter 1, "Neuroses: Depressive and Anxiety Disorders" by J. Mark G. Williams and Isabel R. Hargreaves, addresses various forms of depression and touches on six types of anxiety disorders. In their discussion of depression the authors cover important antecedents and the characteristic symptoms of this disorder. Their treatment section states that cognitive therapy, a technique that involves helping clients to identify and modify distortions in their thinking, is often as effective as antidepressive medication. However, it is important to realize that many people do require medication, and that there are a host of new generation antidepressant drugs, particularly those that increase the level of the neurotransmitter serotonin in the brain. Limitations of space unavoidably truncate their discussion of treatments for anxiety, but the reader will obtain an overall impression of some of the more effective methods. Further details of the present-day treatment of twelve specific disorders including anxiety, depression, eating disorders, and alcoholism can be found in Barlow's (1993) book, *Clinical Handbook of Psychological Disorders: A Step-by-step Treatment Manual*.

In chapter 2, "Psychotic disorders: Schizophrenia, affective psychoses, and paranoia", Chris Frith and Connie Cahill provide a succinct summary of psychotic signs and symptoms, especially the delusions, hallucinations, passivity experiences, and thought disorders related to schizophrenia. The authors refer briefly to manic-depressive psychosis (or affective psychoses), which are often called bipolar mood disorders. They mention the use of lithium carbonate which is widely regarded as the treatment of choice for many bipolar mood disorders. In addition to medication, people suffering from bipolar disorders also often require and respond to cognitive behaviour therapy. The same applies to many schizophrenic disorders, where the proper combination of antipsychotic medication plus effective psychosocial interventions can make a world of difference. We strongly advise the interested reader to consult the book by Mueser and Glynn (1995), *Behavioral Family Therapy for Psychiatric Disorders*. It provides comprehensive and up-to-date accounts of the diagnosis and treatment of psychiatric disorders. We also recommend most highly Bongar and Beutler's (1995) *Comprehensive Textbook of Psychotherapy*.

In chapter 3, "Infantile autism", Simon Baron-Cohen provides a brief summary of one of the most puzzling childhood disorders. The author discusses associated language disorders and social abnormalities, various cognitive mechanisms, and the autistic child's inability to appreciate other people's mental states, which he refers to as "mind-blindness". His chapter concludes with a brief section on treatment of infantile autism. In addition to the further reading that Baron-Cohen has recommended, we would like to mention the excellent book by Schreibman (1988).

In chapter 4, "Eating disorders", Peter J. Cooper discusses anorexia nervosa and bulimia nervosa, provides interesting background information and epidemiological statistics, and discusses important aetiological and treatment considerations. Anorexia nervosa is a life-threatening disorder that predominantly affects young women, especially girls from upper socio-economic families. Their intense fear of gaining weight or becoming fat can literally lead them to starve themselves to death. Bulimia nervosa also has the underlying intent of weight control, but here the person has recurrent episodes of binge eating followed by such compensatory behaviours as self-induced vomiting, misuse of laxatives, fasting, and/or extreme exercise. The treatment of anorexia nervosa usually needs to involve family members and often calls for hospitalization and nursing care. Bulimia nervosa has a better prognosis, and many studies have examined the impact of drugs (for example, certain antidepressants), cognitive behaviour therapy, and interpersonal therapy. As additional reading, we strongly recommend a chapter on eating disorders by Wilson and Pike (1993).

Finally, chapter 5, "Alcohol and drug addiction", by Geoffrey Lowe rounds out this introductory volume on abnormal psychology. The ravages of alcohol addiction and substance abuse throughout our society can hardly be overstated. The suffering, crime, and dire economic consequences of alcoholism and drug addiction are immense. In his chapter, Lowe spells out various models that have been put forth to account for problem drinking – notably the disease model and the social and cognitive learning models. His account of drug addiction also surveys many different factors and concludes that "addictions are best viewed as behaviours developed and maintained by multiple sources". Lowe focuses on different explanatory models but does not comment on treatment approaches. Providing treatment to individuals with drinking problems or drug addiction is a complex process. The clinician is faced with intricate decisions about matching each client to the appropriate level of care, the best treatment setting, and the selection of the necessary treatment modalities and techniques. Every client needs to be assessed and diagnosed in terms of concomitant medical, psychological, psychiatric, and cognitive problems. Again, for additional reading, we recommend the book by Barlow (1993), which contains an outstanding chapter on alcoholism (McCrady, 1993).

All in all, we hope that this book will provide a good sampling of the field of abnormal psychology. The topics that are discussed in the five chapters that follow cover the vast majority of people with mental disorders in our society. We feel that this book will provide students and interested readers with a basic knowledge of some of the most significant mental disorders and may even wet the appetite of some readers to consider pursuing a career in clinical psychology. For those who wish to pursue aspects of abnormal psychology in greater depth, in addition to the books and articles mentioned in this introduction, suggestions for further reading are given at the end of each chapter.

REFERENCES

American Psychiatric Association. (1994). *Diagnostic and statistical manual of mental disorders*. (4th edn.). Washington, DC: American Psychiatric Association.

Barlow, D. H. (ed.). (1993). *Clinical handbook of psychological disorders: A step-by-step treatment manual* (2nd edn). New York: Guilford.

Bongar, B., & Beutler, L. E. (eds). (1995). *Comprehensive textbook of psychotherapy*. Oxford: Oxford University Press.

Davison, G. C., & Neale, J. M. (1994). *Abnormal psychology* (6th edn.). New York: Wiley.

McCrady, B. S. (1993). Alcoholism, in D. H. Barlow (ed.). *Clinical handbook of psychological disorders: A step-by-step treatment manual* (2nd edn.). New York: Guilford, pp. 362–95.

Mueser, K. T., & Glynn, S. (1995). *Behavioral family therapy for psychiatric disorders*. New York: Allyn & Bacon.

Schreibman, L. (1988). *Autism*. Newbury Park, CA: Sage.

Wilson, G. T., & Pike, K. M. (1993). Eating disorders, in D. H. Barlow (ed.). *Clinical handbook of psychological disorders: A step-by-step treatment manual* (2nd edn.). New York: Guilford, pp. 278–317.

NEUROSES: DEPRESSIVE AND ANXIETY DISORDERS

J. Mark G. Williams and Isabel R. Hargreaves

University College of North Wales, Bangor, Wales

People vary in how much they are aware of their emotions, whether these are positive (such as happiness, joy, relaxation) or negative (such as anger, sadness, embarrassment, anxiety). This is partly because any emotion has a number of aspects, and people may feel or express their emotion in a variety of ways. First, there are the *subjective* aspects: we are consciously aware of certain feelings, even if we have difficulty in putting them into words. Second, there are the *behavioural* aspects. People who are anxious may pace up and down; people who are angry may clench their fists; people who are in despair may cry or hang their heads. Third, there are *bodily* aspects. The body undergoes various changes when an emotion is experienced. These may include changes in heart-rate, in muscle tension, in rate of perspiration (measured by small changes in electrical resistance across the surface of the skin), and in the electrical patterns in the brain (measured by electroencephalogram or EEG). Finally, there are the *cognitive* aspects. The ways in which the mind processes what is happening in the world and in the body (the perception, encoding, storage, and retrieval of information) becomes biased by emotional states. We shall see how such biases give rise to distortions in thinking, which cause even more emotional disturbance and further biased processing. That is, a vicious circle is set up from which it is difficult to escape. If this biasing has existed from childhood (often because of early stress), it gives rise to fixed attitudes and beliefs about oneself (e.g., "I am a failure") or about relationships ("No one would love me if they really knew me").

In this chapter, we shall describe the two most common emotional disorders: depressive and anxiety neuroses. The point at which normal emotion becomes abnormal is difficult to define. Anxiety and depression are a part of everyday living. It is only when they persist and become more severe that they cause problems for people or their families. We shall describe how symptoms of depression and anxiety tend to cluster together into different categories; and how a psychological understanding has helped in the development of new treatments.

DEPRESSION

DEPRESSION AND ITS SYMPTOMS

The term "depression" is used very often in our day-by-day conversation to describe a normal downswing of mood. Such downswings in mood may be adaptive. They may remind of losses and spur a person to find ways of re-engaging with activities or friends. But if the depression becomes more prolonged, it begins to cause more problems than it solves. Such people ruminate on negative themes, brooding about past unpleasantness and feeling pessimistic about the future. They feel resentful, irritable, or angry much of the time, feeling sorry for themselves, and constantly needing reassurance from someone.

If depression deepens still further, more symptoms are drawn in. These symptoms include further emotional changes (feelings of extreme sadness and hopelessness) cognitive changes (low self-esteem, guilt, memory and

2

Table 1 Symptoms of clinical depression

In order to be said to be suffering from clinical depression, a number of the following symptoms need to have occurred together over a period of time

A Persistent low mood (for at least two weeks)

   plus

B At least five of the following symptoms

1 Poor appetite or weight loss, or increased appetite or weight gain (change of 1 lb a week over several weeks or 10 lb in a year when not dieting)
2 Sleep difficulty or sleeping too much
3 Loss of energy, fatigability, or tiredness
4 Body slowed down or agitated (not mere subjective feeling of restlessness or being slowed down but observable by others)
5 Loss of interest or pleasure in usual activities, including social contact or sex
6 Feelings of self-reproach, excessive or inappropriate guilt
7 Complaints or evidence of diminished ability to think or concentrate such as slowed thinking or indecisiveness
8 Recurrent thoughts of death or suicide, or any suicidal behaviour

Source: Spitzer, Endicott, and Robins, 1978

concentration difficulties); changes in behaviour (feeling agitated or slowed down, reduced interest in social or recreational activities) and bodily changes (sleep, eating, and sexual problems, aches and pains, loss of energy).

If the depression is intense enough to include five or more of the symptoms shown in Table 1 occurring together for more than a two-week period, it is usually thought to be a "clinical depression" which might benefit from some sort of psychological or medical help. At any one time, there are some 5 per cent of the population who are clinically depressed. Of these episodes of depression, 25 per cent last less than a month; a further 50 per cent recover in less than three months. However, depression tends to return, and within two years of recovering from one episode, around three-quarters will have suffered another episode of depression.

SEX DIFFERENCES IN DEPRESSION

Women are between two and three times as likely to become clinically depressed as are men. The reasons for this remain uncertain. Women with young children are particularly vulnerable; this has led some to suggest that women's disadvantaged role with regard to opportunities for paid employment and their increased responsibility for unpaid child-care is the major cause. The correlation between onset of depression, increase in life stress, and the absence of social support (Brown, 1989) supports this conclusion.

What is less clear is whether women are more vulnerable than men if they

3

have never been depressed before. A large study in the United States surveyed 1,000 people in the community over an eight month period (Amenson & Lewinsohn, 1981). It found, as others have before and since, that depression was more common in women than men. But because the researchers followed the same people for a long period (rather than just taking a "snapshot" as other studies had done), they could count what proportion of men and women became depressed *for the first time* during the period of the study. Their results showed a balance between the sexes: 7.1 per cent of the men and 6.9 per cent of the women became depressed for the first time.

This implies that the sex difference arises because women who have had one episode of depression are more likely to become depressed again than are men who have had a similar episode. Of those women who had been depressed before the study began, 22 per cent became depressed again during the study, but only 13 per cent of men who had been depressed before became depressed again. We need to explain not the increased vulnerability of women to a single episode of depression, but their increased vulnerability to repeated episodes following a first episode. We have already mentioned the stresses and potential loneliness of a child-care role. This is clearly important. Another possibility is that the hormonal changes of a woman's menstrual cycle, though not enough to bring about clinical depression by itself, may nevertheless tend to reactivate memories and attitudes from a previous period of major depression once this has occurred for other reasons.

DISTINCTIONS BETWEEN DIFFERENT SORTS OF DEPRESSION

Many attempts have been made to identify different types of depression. The distinction that has aroused most controversy, yet become most firmly embedded within psychiatric thinking, is that between *endogenous* and *reactive* depressions. The term "endogenous" was originally intended to describe those whose depression arose "from the inside" (from biochemical disturbances in the brain). These were thought to be different from "reactive depression": those who were depressed because of some external stresses. Yet there are many more differences between "endogenous" and "reactive" depression than simply whether the person had been under stress. Indeed, it has been found that endogenous depression is preceded by stressful events as often as reactive depression (Paykel, 1989). The term "endogenous" (also called "biological" depression) is now used to describe a certain cluster of symptoms (see Table 2), and not to refer to how the depression was caused.

Table 2   Symptoms of endogenous-type depression

From group A and B a total of at least six symptoms are required before a definite diagnosis of endogenous-type depression is made; these six must include at least one symptom from group A

A   1   Distinct quality to depressed mood, that is, depressed mood is perceived as distinctly different from the kind of feeling (s)he would have or has had following the death of a loved one
    2   Lack of reactivity to environmental changes (once depressed doesn't feel better, even temporarily, when something good happens)
    3   Mood is regularly worse in the morning
    4   Loss of interest or pleasure which affects everything

B   1   Feelings of self-reproach or excessive or inappropriate guilt
    2   Early morning wakening or insomnia in the middle of the night
    3   Body is slowed down or agitated (more than mere subjective feeling of being slowed down or restless; rather the changes are large enough for others to notice)
    4   Poor appetite
    5   Weight loss (2 lb a week over several weeks or 20 lb in a year when not dieting)
    6   Loss of interest or pleasure in usual activities or decreased sexual drive

Source: Spitzer, Endicott, and Robins, 1978

PSYCHOLOGICAL THEORIES OF DEPRESSION

In order to deal effectively with depression, it is important to know what psychological factors may be causing and maintaining it. Two of the most prominent theories will be mentioned: first, that depression is caused and maintained by people's poor social skills, so that they become isolated from friends and family; and second, that depression is caused and maintained by negative attitudes and thoughts.

Problems in relating to others

Do depressed patients have problems in relating to others: do they have problems in their "social skills"? Early research seemed to show that depressed patients had problems in a number of areas including the extent to which they distribute their attention evenly around a group, slowness in responding to what another person has said, and the small number of times they "reward" other people with attentiveness and smiles. However, subsequent research has revealed a paradox. Depressed patients rate themselves (and are rated by others) as being socially unskilled. But when attempts are made to measure precisely what this social awkwardness might be, the evidence for it is weak. So how is it that patients and observers agree that there is something wrong with their social behaviour?

5

The question has been partly answered in a series of studies on the effect that a depressed person's behaviour has on other people. In one such study, psychologists recorded conversations between undergraduates and depressed patients. These were compared with conversations with patients who were not depressed (Coyne, 1976). They did not find any difference in the social skills of the depressed patients compared with non-depressed patients. However, when the undergraduates were asked about their own feelings after the conversations, they said that they felt more depressed, anxious, and hostile following the conversations with depressed patients than after the conversation with non-depressed patients. They were also more likely to say that they did not want any future contact with the depressed individuals. When the authors analysed the content of the depressed people's conversation, it was found that they spent more time giving personal information about themselves than the non-depressed person: they talked freely of deaths, marital infidelities, hysterectomies, family strife, and so on. It seems that the conversation of people when depressed may have an alienating effect on the person to whom they are talking. Early sympathy for the person is replaced by feelings of "not wanting to know" because of the depressing effect it has on the listener. The depressed person needs others to listen but may find that fewer and fewer people are available, which simply increases the feeling of desperation (see Figure 1).

So depressed people may find themselves (because of what they talk about) more often in situations that would exceed most people's capacities. It is

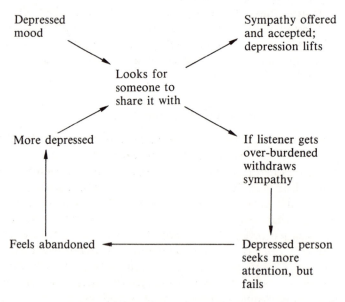

Figure 1   The effect of depression on other people: a vicious circle

hardly surprising that they withdraw altogether from such situations. If this is the case, the important thing for therapy to tackle is not social skills, but the person's negative and self-blameful way of thinking and talking to others. The second theory about the cause and maintenance of depression focuses on this negative attitude.

Depression and cognitive bias

We mentioned at the outset how emotion could affect the way information is processed. An important aspect of this is retrieval from memory. Many depressed people have had a number of stresses and traumas in their lives. Normally, people are quite adept at forgetting unpleasant things about the past. Depression reverses this tendency. As if it was not bad enough to remember the bad things that have happened, depression makes things even worse by reducing the person's ability to recall any good things that have occurred. Looking back on their lives, depressed people may see nothing but a series of disappointments and failures.

Researchers have studied this reversal by measuring the time taken to recall pleasant and unpleasant personal experiences (Lloyd & Lishman, 1975). Depressed patients were given common words as cues (e.g., table, house, wall) and asked to recall either a pleasant or unpleasant memory to each

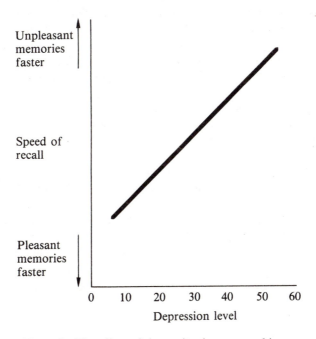

Figure 2   The effect of depression in memory biases

7

word. The ratio of time taken to recall unpleasant memories to the time taken to recall pleasant memories was calculated for each patient (see Figure 2). The results clearly showed that the more severe the depression the quicker the patient recalled an unpleasant memory relative to a pleasant memory.

That these results were not due to the more depressed patients having had more negative experiences in their life was shown by another study by Clark and Teasdale (1982) in Oxford. In this study, patients were asked about their memories when their mood was very low, and again when their depression was not so severe. They were again given words as cues and asked to respond with the first memory that came to mind. The results showed that happy memories were less probable and depressing memories more probable when patients were more depressed. This confirmed how the change in memory processes due to mood shifts may maintain depression by making the past seem even worse than it is (Clark & Teasdale, 1982).

What is the long-term effect of such bias? If a person has, since childhood, tended to recall unpleasant aspects of situations, then this will affect the way *new* events are explained. Successes will be discounted ("It was just good luck, the task was easy"). Failure will be seen as typical ("This confirms how useless I am"). Indeed, many researchers have found that people who are prone to depression differ in how they interpret events in just these ways. When an unpleasant event occurs, they attribute the cause to themselves (internal) rather than to other people or circumstances (external); and to factors that are unlikely to change (stable), rather than to changeable factors (unstable). Finally, they attribute the cause of the event to factors that affect a great many areas of their lives (global) rather than to factors that have only a restricted relevance (specific). For example, if depressed people fail an examination, they would tend to say that it was because they did not have the necessary ability (an internal, stable attribution) rather than that this particular examination was very difficult (external, unstable). Furthermore, they say that it is not just this particular subject at which they are poor, but that they are unsuccessful in exams in general. In this case they have made a global rather than a specific attribution. In the most extreme cases, they may conclude not only that all future attempts to take examinations will be hopeless but also that they are a failure as a person. It is not difficult to see that people who make attributions for failure to internal, stable, and global causes will tend to give up, will become more depressed, and might feel that it is not worth continuing with their education. If they make similar sorts of attributions in other areas of their lives (see Table 3), this will further increase their sense of despair and hopelessness about the future.

Table 3 First reactions

The different ways in which people interpret the same event can be assessed by asking for first reactions. The following items are taken from a questionnaire called the "Cognitive Style Test" by Ivy-Marie Blackburn. Look at these descriptions of everyday events. Imagine they are happening to you. What would your first reaction be?

You are unable to deal with a problem at work and have to ask for help

Would you think

(a)   I often find it difficult to cope with problems
(b)   I find it difficult to cope with some problems
(c)   I am a failure
(d)   These sorts of problems are always easier with help

A person you admire tells you he/she likes you

Would you think

(a)   I am glad she/he likes me
(b)   People sometimes say that without really meaning it
(c)   I am a very likeable person
(d)   I cannot believe that I am likeable

Now ask yourself how your reaction might have been different if you were overtired, or feeling down? How might it affect what you would do next? Psychologists have found that mood dramatically affects the way people interpret ambiguous events, causing further mood changes, and affecting how people behave (see Blackburn, 1987).

Source: Based on Blackburn, 1987

PSYCHOLOGICAL TREATMENT FOR DEPRESSION

Distortions in thinking which occur in people who are emotionally disturbed cannot be changed simply by telling them that they are wrong. New methods of treatment, called collectively "cognitive therapy", give guidelines on how to deal with the negative "self-propaganda" (thoughts, memories, and beliefs) that maintain depression and make the person vulnerable to future episodes. Cognitive techniques aim first at making patients reconceptualize their thoughts and memories as *simply* thoughts and memories which may have been susceptible to distortion, rather than as reflecting reality. It does this in three ways:

1 by eliciting the patient's thoughts, "self-talk", and interpretations of events (e.g., "I failed that exam because I am stupid");
2 by gathering, with the patient, evidence for or against the interpretation (e.g., "Are there any other reasons why I might have failed – e.g., difficult

exam, didn't revise correct material, ill on the day?" "Does failure in this subject imply that I am stupid?");

3 by setting up "experiments" (homeworks) to test out the truth of the interpretations and gather more data for discussion (Find out if others also failed; how do the teachers/lecturers explain what happened? Are resits allowed? What is the procedure for this?).

The major techniques used in cognitive therapy are listed in Table 4, together with a brief description of their purpose.

Many studies have shown that such cognitive therapy techniques are effective in reducing depression (Williams, 1992). They do so as rapidly and as effectively as antidepressant medication. They are more costly than drugs in the short term because each patient sees a therapist for an hour a week for up to 15 weeks, but cognitive therapy is suitable for those patients who cannot or do not want to take medication. More importantly, the chances of the depression returning following cognitive therapy are significantly lower than following antidepressant medication, so it may be better in the long term. These advances in the treatment of depression show the importance of understanding the psychological processes underlying such emotional problems, a theme which emerges strongly in the second emotion we discuss, namely anxiety.

Table 4 Five core techniques of cognitive therapy

Technique	Purpose
Thought catching	To teach the person to become aware of depressing thoughts as they occur
Task assignment	To encourage activities which the person has been avoiding (e.g., meeting a certain friend, attending a meeting of a club or society)
Reality testing	To select tasks which help to test out the truth of fixed negative thoughts or beliefs (e.g., phoning a friend to test out the idea that "no one will talk to me")
Cognitive rehearsal	To get the person to recount to the therapist all the stages involved in an activity he or she has been avoiding, together with the accompanying thoughts and feelings; the aim is to discover possible "roadblocks", what can be done about them, and to imagine eventual success
Alternative therapy	To instruct the person to imagine an upsetting situation and then generate strategies for coping

ANXIETY

ANXIETY AND ITS SYMPTOMS

Anxiety, like depression, is a normal part of everyday life for the majority of people. It serves the useful function of keeping us motivated to make the effort to overcome threatening situations. Take, for example, the common experience of becoming anxious prior to an interview. The fear that we shall do badly means that we work hard to prepare for it. However, it is also a common experience that anxiety can lead to worse performance. In other words, anxiety can become handicapping.

In evolutionary terms, anxiety can be viewed as a mechanism that has enabled animals and humans to deal with danger and threat. If an animal comes across a predator, a *survival reaction* occurs. Its body undergoes physiological changes which increase arousal levels, enabling enhanced performance to increase the chances of survival, either to stay and fight the threatening animal or to take rapid flight, the *fight/flight mechanism*.

The difference between adaptive anxiety and pathological anxiety is in the identification of threat. Whereas in adaptive anxiety the threat is all too clear (being mauled by a bear or the possibility of failing an exam), in pathological anxiety the threat is often either unidentified (the sufferer is only aware of fear, not what is feared) or out of proportion (for example, a fear of being embarrassed) or irrational (for example, anxiety about being severely ill despite all reassurance).

The result is that the bodily changes of the survival reaction occur in situations where there is no danger. Many of these symptoms are caused by the release of adrenaline (epinephrine) from the adrenal medulla located just at the top of the kidneys. On perception of threat, whether real or imagined, adrenaline is released into the body in order to allow the survival reaction to occur. All the symptoms of anxiety are by-products of bodily changes that would enhance performance in situations of real threat (see Figure 3). The problem with clinical anxiety is that because the threat is ill perceived, the anxious individual, for lack of an alternative focus, concentrates on bodily symptoms and discomforts. The symptoms of anxiety can be exceedingly unpleasant and frightening in themselves, and many people naturally conclude that there is something physically wrong with them. We shall list the symptoms first, then describe how they cluster together to form definable syndromes. Finally we shall describe how psychologists have approached anxiety and its treatment.

Symptoms of anxiety

The symptoms of anxiety are very diverse: dizziness, lightheadedness, blurred vision, hot flushes, dry mouth, tightness in the throat (often accompanied by a feeling of choking), muscular tension and pains, breathing difficulties, a pounding, racing heart, feelings of nausea, butterflies in the tummy, numbness in the limbs, pins and needles in the extremities, the urge to urinate and defecate, feeling cold, hot flushes, sweating, twitching, trembling, shaking, symptoms of vigilance and scanning such as feeling on edge, exaggerated startle response, poor concentration, trouble falling/staying asleep, and irritability. The number of symptoms and the severity varies from individual

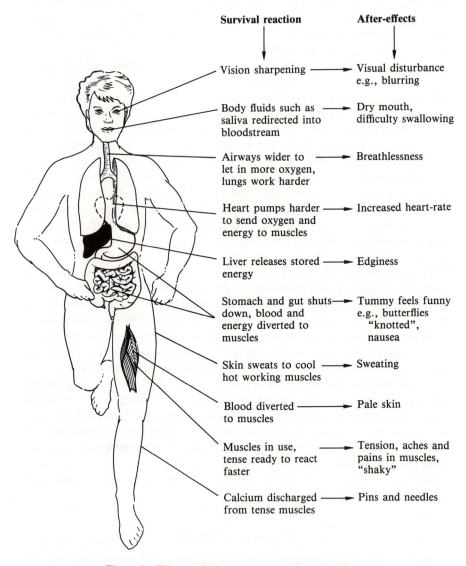

Figure 3   The survival reaction and its after-effects

to individual. We shall now describe how these symptoms cluster together to form some of the more common problems, starting with the most common, generalized anxiety disorder.

COMMON TYPES OF ANXIETY DISORDERS

Generalized anxiety disorder

Generalized anxiety disorder is usually characterized by severe and disproportionate worry about life issues which persists more or less consistently for 6 or more months. In any one year, between 2 and 6.5 per cent of the general population suffer from generalized anxiety disorder. This makes it the most common form of anxiety neurosis. The most common forms of worry seem to be related to family issues (79 per cent in one study); over-concern about finances (50 per cent); work (43 per cent); and personal illness (14 per cent) (see Edelmann, 1992). In addition, most people report worrying about many other little things. As well as these worries, the anxious person shows muscle tension, hyperactivity in the autonomic nervous system (e.g., sweating), and is apprehensive for much of the time. Information processing is biased, but instead of the main bias being in memory (as in depression), the main problem is bias in attention. People are apt to be hypervigilant, scanning their environment for anything that might be a threat (Williams, Watts, Macleod, & Mathews, 1988).

Several experiments have demonstrated this hypervigilance in people who are anxious. In one study, mothers who were anxious because their children were soon to go into hospital to have their tonsils out were tested (Parkinson & Rachman, 1981). They listened to a tape recording of music in which were hidden words, recorded very quietly under the music. The words were either neutral (e.g. *newspaper*, *bird*) or threatening (*operation*, *bleeding*). Other women, whose children were not undergoing an operation, also listened to the tape. The results showed that, even when the unpleasant words were played at their quietest volume so that the other women could not hear them, the anxious mothers could hear them. This hypervigilance has been called "perceptual pop-out", and works for vision as well as for hearing (see Figure 4). Shortly after the operation, these mothers' attentional systems returned to normal. In severe anxiety states, however, the person suffers from such a bias almost all the time.

Panic disorder

Panic disorder is a more extreme form of anxiety than that found in generalized anxiety disorder. Panic disorder consists of recurrent panic attacks: time limited periods of extreme fear/discomfort. Panic attacks might last for a few minutes or, rarely, several hours. They usually occur unexpectedly, although

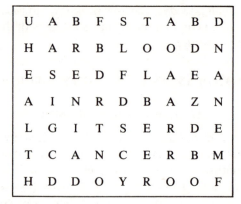

Figure 4 Perceptual pop-out. Anxious people may see threat words more quickly than non-threat words in an array of letters such as this

associations with situations and places may eventually develop, for example, crowded supermarkets. Such associations increase the likelihood of further panic attacks occurring because they are expected to happen. Any of the physical symptoms associated with anxiety can be experienced during a panic attack but at least four of the symptoms listed in Table 5 must be present for panic disorder to be diagnosed.

Panic attacks are very common in the general population. One study found that 34 per cent of young, normal adults experience an isolated panic attack in any twelve-month period. However, full-blown panic disorder is much rarer, estimated as being between 0.5 and 3 per cent in the general population.

Agoraphobia

Clinically, panic disorder is often associated with agoraphobia (fear of being in places or situations from which escape might be difficult). The literal

Table 5 Symptoms that may occur in panic disorder

Shortness of breath
Palpitations or accelerated heart-rate
Chest pain or discomfort
Choking or smothering sensations
Dizziness, unsteady feelings, or faintness
Trembling or shakiness
Tingling sensations
Sweating and hot and cold flushes
Fear of dying, going crazy, or doing something uncontrollable

meaning of the word "agoraphobia" is fear (Greek *phobos*) of the market-place (Greek *agora*). More generally, agoraphobia includes fear of busy streets, travelling on buses, trains, or cars, and standing in queues. It is now recognized that the onset and maintenance of agoraphobia is often due to the occurrence of panic attacks, and that these should be the primary focus of therapy.

Social phobia

Social phobia is the persistent fear of one or more social situations in which the individual feels exposed to the scrutiny of others. The fear then becomes one of embarrassing oneself. Social phobia includes fears such as speaking in public, eating in public, urinating in public conveniences, or writing in the presence of others. More general fears are of saying foolish things and being unable to respond to queries. The socially phobic individual usually avoids such situations wherever possible. In its mildest forms, social anxiety is very common. One UK study found 10 per cent of students had difficulty in or avoided social situations, and another US study put the figure at one-third. However, a social phobia of clinical proportions is rare, the prevalence in the general population being around 1 per cent.

Simple phobia

In simple phobia, the feared object is usually clearly defined: a fear of spiders, birds, snakes, mice, blood, closed spaces (claustrophobia), heights (acrophobia), or air travel. Being in the presence of the feared object produces the anxiety response but at all other times the person's anxiety level is normal. Because of this, and because the phobic object is often relatively easy to avoid, simple phobias are rarely handicapping. Surveys have reported that between 6 and 8 per cent of the general population report phobias but only 2 per cent of these find them disabling (Agras, Sylvester, & Oliveau, 1969).

Obsessive-compulsive disorder

Obsessive-compulsive disorder is characterized by persistent ideas, impulses, or images that are intrusive, seemingly useless and often distressing, and that interfere with daily life or relationships. Examples include the intrusive impulse of killing a much-loved child, shouting out swear-words in church, or thoughts to do with violence, contamination, and doubt. Compulsions are repetitive and apparently purposeless actions performed in a stereotyped fashion. For example, having to do things in a particular rigid sequence, repeatedly checking things, frequently handwashing, counting, and touching objects. The action usually serves the purpose of reducing anxiety and

15

tension. It is not experienced as pleasurable, but resistance to a compulsion leads to mounting tension and anxiety. Studies show that up to 2.5 per cent of the population have suffered from this disorder at some point in their lives. In any six-month period, 1.5 per cent of the population can be found to have obsessive compulsive disorder. Men are equally likely to have the disorder as women, though the nature of the symptoms differ (see Edelmann, 1992). Women are more likely to be compulsive cleaners (86 per cent of compulsive cleaners are women). By contrast compulsive checkers are more likely to be men (73 per cent).

Post-traumatic stress disorder

Post-traumatic stress disorder (PTSD) is somewhat different from the rest of the anxiety disorders described so far. It is essentially a normal reaction to an abnormal situation. Symptoms develop following a highly distressing event, such as a threat to one's life (or the life of loved ones), the destruction of one's home/community, witnessing the death of others as the result of accident or physical violence, rape/assault, wartime experience, or torture. Typically in PTSD, the event is re-experienced in a number of ways. For example, the individual may experience intrusive thoughts and images relating to the event, dissociative states during which the event is re-lived, intense psychological distress as a result of other factors associated with the event (such as anniversaries, places), and recurrent nightmares about the event. Typically the PTSD sufferers will avoid circumstances associated with the trauma. However, sometimes PTSD can include amnesia for the event and feeling emotionally detached from the world. It is difficult to estimate how many people develop PTSD following a trauma, but some studies have found that up to 15 per cent do so. The proportion is higher in children, varying from 30 to 50 per cent (Yule, 1991).

PSYCHOLOGICAL THEORIES OF ANXIETY

We turn now to describe the two most commonly used theories and successful treatments of anxiety in psychology, the behavioural and cognitive approaches.

Behavioural theory

The behavioural theory of anxiety states that anxiety is a learned or classically conditioned response, produced at first by the association of fear with a certain situation/object. The second stage is finding that escaping from the situation produces relief. The final stage is the avoidance of anxiety by avoiding the particular situation or object altogether. Some psychologists have suggested that anxiety disorders may start as conditioned responses but

16

then produce more obvious rewards and/or solve another problem. For example, an agoraphobic sufferer might find that the disorder produces benefits such as greater amounts of attention from an otherwise inattentive partner. If the agoraphobia is reduced, and the person becomes more independent, this change sometimes leads to a different and possibly more distressing problem such as interpersonal difficulties. Indeed, one study found that improving agoraphobic problems can lead to marital disharmony (Barlow, Mavissakalian, & Kay 1981).

Cognitive theory

The cognitive theory of anxiety disorders focuses on the thoughts individuals have about themselves, their symptoms, and the situations they are in. Pathologically anxious people are likely to make certain errors in thinking that lead them to overestimate the degree of danger/threat and underestimate their own ability to cope and the presence of rescue factors within the threatening situation. These errors are: catastrophization (fearing the worst will happen), personalization (assuming personal significance in negative events), over-generalizing (assuming one negative event will affect everything), selective abstraction (taking one negative element and drawing negative conclusions), minimization (denying the importance of good events/coping skills) and maximization (exaggerating importance of negative events/non-adaptive skills).

For example, research on the cause of panic attacks by David Clark (1986) and his colleagues in Oxford has shown that panic attacks are the result of misinterpreting, in a catastrophic way, bodily reactions associated with anxiety such as increased heart-rate or dizziness. A person notices an increase in heart-rate (a normal symptom of anxiety which can cause no harm) and immediately concludes that he or she is about to suffer a fatal heart attack. The acute anxiety that this thought naturally creates causes further bodily symptoms (such as further increases in heart-rate) which serves only to confirm the initial "diagnosis". Such misinterpretations invariably lead to a further exacerbation of symptoms and hence a full-blown panic attack occurs (see Figure 5).

The proposal that catastrophic interpretations of bodily symptoms lead to panic attacks has had support from an experiment conducted by David Clark and his colleagues in Oxford (Clark et al. 1991). Panic patients were given sodium lactate, which has the effect of inducing symptoms very similar to those experienced during an attack. Patients were randomly assigned to two groups. Prior to the infusion of sodium lactate, all patients were told that sodium lactate is harmless and induces a specific set of symptoms and that they could stop the infusion at any time. One group were told no more than this. The other group were told that the sensations induced were similar to those produced by exercise or alcohol, that lactate is a natural substance produced by the body, that it was normal to experience intense sensations

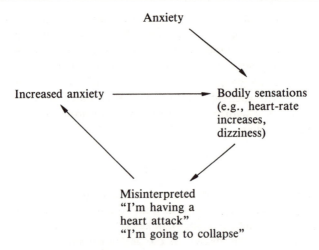

Figure 5   Vicious circle of anxiety and panic

during the infusion, and that these did not indicate an adverse reaction. The experimenters took measures of heart-rate, blood pressure, skin conduct-ance, respiration rate, and anxiety self-ratings, before and throughout the infusion. Above all, the investigators wanted to know whether a panic attack had occurred or not so they arranged for an independent investigator to inter-view the patients about their experiences during the experiment. They found that very few of the patients who had been given the alternative explanation for their symptoms had a panic attack. By contrast, in the group that had been allowed to interpret their symptoms in their own (catastrophic) way, all patients experienced a panic attack during the infusion. These findings give very strong and compelling evidence in favour of a cognitive theory of panic disorder. They have led to the development of very effective techniques for treating panic and associated disorders. We shall describe some of these below, after mentioning several techniques that developed from behavioural theories.

PSYCHOLOGICAL TREATMENTS FOR ANXIETY

Behavioural treatment

One of the earliest behavioural treatment techniques was developed by Joseph Wolpe (1958) and is called systematic desensitization by reciprocal inhibition. Phobic patients are gradually faced with increasingly fearful and threatening situations or objects (either in actuality or imaginally) while at the same time putting into practice previously trained relaxation techniques. The theory behind this very successful technique was that by pairing the feared

18

situation/object with a state of relaxation a new association is created and the anxiety reaction is inhibited from occurring. Others have argued that this technique works not because of the inhibiting effect of relaxation on anxiety but because of the exposure to the feared situation (Marks, 1973). Generally it is now assumed that the key to overcoming anxiety is through confronting or facing the fear. Exposure is the most effective way to achieve this – especially if it allows the person to disprove any predictions he or she is making that something awful will happen. Therapists usually use a gradual technique (graded exposure), building up the feared situations from week to week as therapy progresses. At the same time, the patient's sense of confidence to cope with exposure increases.

Cognitive treatment

The cognitive treatment of anxiety disorders involves tackling the way in which individuals think about the threatening situation (including their bodily symptoms) and how this affects the way they behave (see Beck & Emery, 1985). For example, as mentioned above, people with panic symptoms believe that if the panic attack is not curtailed rapidly, they will suffer from some physical catastrophe, so they attempt to escape the panic-provoking situation as soon as possible (Clark, 1986). Once escape has occurred, individuals lose the opportunity to establish whether their beliefs are justified or not since they are no longer able to put them to the test. The act of escaping leads to further faulty beliefs such as: "If I hadn't sat down I would definitely have fainted" or "If I hadn't got out I would definitely have had a fatal heart attack".

Like cognitive treatment for depression (see above) the treatment for anxiety aims initially to help the client to identify and recognize these thoughts and evaluate their influence on behaviour. Clients can then examine their status in the world of reality. Once these thoughts have been identified they can be re-evaluated and re-interpreted along more realistic lines. This impacts differently on the behaviour with the effect that the client is more able to cope with exposure to the feared situation. This gives the person further opportunity to discover that the predictions he or she was previously making were faulty.

CONCLUSION

This chapter has concentrated on anxiety and depression as problems in their own right, but it is important to realize that they occur in many other situations where people are disturbed or upset. Where they are present, one often finds that they cause avoidance of certain activities, which can then lead to further problems. Following bereavement, for example, some people find

19

that even months afterwards, when they would like to be able to deal with the person's belongings, they cannot do so. If grief becomes "blocked" in this way, a combination of "cognitive rehearsal" and "graded exposure" can be used. The person first imagines him or herself going into that situation. Second, the person generates ways of coping with difficulties that might arise. Third, the person imagines as clearly as possible the potential benefits. Finally, the person sets a definite time when he or she is going to start the task, including a plan for what to do immediately afterwards.

Another way in which the ideas mentioned here have been extended is to help understand the attributional distortions in schoolchildren who persistently fail at reading or mathematics despite the fact that their level of intelligence should enable them to succeed. When they find work difficult, these children attribute their failure to internal, stable, and global factors, for example, that they are "stupid and incapable". Simply giving them experience of success to increase their self-esteem does not work. Psychologists found that this was because it did not teach them how to deal with failure (Dweck, 1975). They suggested instead that the children be allowed to fail as part of their remedial training so that their distorted attributions are made explicit and can be changed. The children were encouraged to think aloud as they attempted to do their work. When failure occurred, rather than seeing this as evidence of incompetence, the children were encouraged to interpret it as arising from things that could be changed (e.g., "I went too quickly", "I didn't concentrate hard enough in the middle"). The results showed that when the children met difficulty again in the real classroom, they persisted for longer and were more likely to succeed. The children had learned to cope with failure.

Psychological factors are important in determining the onset and course of anxiety and depression in many ways. First, habitual tendencies to interpret situations in a negative or threatening way can render the person vulnerable to stressors, such as a threatening life-event or a physical illness. Second, the psychological factors can act as precipitants which raise the level of stress experienced when a negative event occurs. Third, psychological factors contribute to the maintenance of emotional disturbance whatever the cause of the initial disturbance. Knowledge of underlying psychological processes have contributed much to the alleviation of these conditions. Note that "exposure" is an important element in the treatment of both depression and anxiety. However, in the case of anxiety, the emphasis has changed from focusing on the unpleasantness of the external environment to the fear of the internal environment, that is, bodily reactions. In both depression and anxiety, the emphasis has changed away from focusing on reactions to events in the world and towards how these events are interpreted.

FURTHER READING

Blackburn, I. M. (1987). *Coping with depression*. Edinburgh: Chambers.

Edelmann, R. J. (1992). *Anxiety: Theory, research and intervention in clinical and health psychology*. Chichester: Wiley.

Gotlib, I. H., & Hammen, C. L. (1992). *Psychological aspects of depression: Toward a cognitive interpersonal integration*. Chichester: Wiley.

Last, C., & Hersen, M. (Eds) (1987). *Handbook of anxiety disorders*. New York: Pergamon.

Williams, J. M. G. (1992). *The psychological treatment of depression: A guide to the theory and practice of cognitive behaviour therapy* (2nd edn). London: Routledge.

REFERENCES

Agras, W. S., Sylvester, D., & Oliveau, D. (1969). The epidemiology of common fears and phobia. *Comprehensive Psychiatry*, *10*, 151–161.

Amenson, C. S., & Lewinsohn, P. M. (1981). An investigation into the observed sex differences in prevalence of unipolar depression. *Journal of Abnormal Psychology*, *90*, 1–13.

Barlow, D., Mavissakalian, M., & Kay, L. (1981). Couples treatment of agoraphobia: Changes in marital satisfaction. *Behaviour Research and Therapy*, *19*, 245–255.

Barlow, D., O'Brien, G., & Last, C. (1988). Couples treatment of agoraphobia. *Behaviour Therapy*, *15*, 41–58.

Beck, A. T., & Emery, G. (1985). *Anxiety disorders and phobias*. New York: Basic Books.

Blackburn, I. M. (1987). *Coping with depression*. Edinburgh: Chambers.

Brown, G. W. (1989). Depression: A radical social perspective. In K. Herbst & E. S. Paykel (Eds) *Depression: An integrative approach* (pp. 21–44). Oxford: Heinemann Medical.

Clark, D. M. (1986). A cognitive approach to panic. *Behaviour Research and Therapy*, *24*, 461–470.

Clark, D. M., & Teasdale, J. D. (1982). Diurnal variation in clinical depression and accessibility of positive and negative experiences. *Journal of Abnormal Psychology*, *91*, 87–95.

Clark, D. M., Salkovskis, P. M., Gelder, M. G., Middleton, H., Anastasiades, P., & Hackmann, A. (1991). *Cognitive mediation of lactate induced panic*. Paper presented at the annual conference of the American Psychological Association, Washington, DC, August.

Coyne, J. C. (1976). Depression and the response of others. *Journal of Abnormal Psychology*, *85*, 186–193.

Dweck, C. S. (1975). The role of expectations and attributions in the alleviation of learned helplessness. *Journal of Personality and Social Psychology*, *31*, 674–685.

Edelmann, R. J. (1992). *Anxiety: Theory, research and intervention in clinical and health psychology*. Chichester: Wiley.

Lloyd, G. C., & Lishman, W. A. (1975). Effect of depression on the speed of recall of pleasant and unpleasant experiences. *Psychological Medicine*, *5*, 173–180.

Marks, I. M. (1973). The reduction of fear: Towards a unifying theory. *Journal of the Canadian Psychiatric Association*, *18*, 9–12.

Parkinson, L., & Rachman, S. (1981). Intrusive thoughts: The effects of an uncontrived stress. *Advances in Behaviour Research & Therapy*, *3*, 111–118.

Paykel, E. S. (1989). The background: Extent and nature of the disorder. In K. Herbst & E. S. Paykel (Eds) *Depression: An integrative approach* (pp. 3–20). London: Heinemann.

Spitzer, R. L., Endicott, J., & Robins, E. (1978). *Research Diagnostic Criteria (RDC) for a selected group of functional disorders* (3rd edn). New York: New York State Psychiatric Institute, Biometrics Research.

Williams, J. M. G. (1992). *The psychological treatment of depression: A guide to the theory and practice of cognitive behaviour therapy* (2nd edn). London: Routledge.

Williams, J. M. G., Watts, F. N., MacLeod, C., & Mathews, A. (1988). *Cognitive psychology and emotional disorders*. Chichester: Wiley.

Wolpe, J. (1958). *Psychotherapy by reciprocal inhibition*. Stanford, CA: Stanford University Press.

Yule, W. (1991). Working with children following disasters. In M. Herbert (Ed.), *Clinical child psychology* (pp. 349–364). Chichester: Wiley.

2

PSYCHOTIC DISORDERS: SCHIZOPHRENIA, AFFECTIVE PSYCHOSES, AND PARANOIA

Chris Frith and Connie Cahill

MRC Cyclotron Unit and University College London, England

Psychosis is the technical term for what non-psychologists call madness. In contrast to the symptoms of neurosis, psychotic symptoms are categorically outside the normal realm of experience, and as such they are beyond our common-sense powers of understanding and empathy. It is this aspect of psychotic symptoms that isolates persons experiencing them in "a world of their own". Schizophrenia is by far the most common of the psychoses. The lifetime risk of having a schizophrenic breakdown is estimated at between 0.5 per cent and 2 per cent; the risk for affective psychosis lies between approximately 0.6 per cent and 1.1 per cent. These disorders frequently strike in early adulthood, the average age of onset for schizophrenia being around 25 years in males and 30 years in females (Johnstone, 1991). The personal, social, and economic costs of these illnesses are great. Sufferers stand to lose their relationships, their jobs or careers, their homes, and ultimately their freedom. Families can be emotionally devastated by the shock of the changes wrought on their relative, as well as having to cope with the person's uncharacteristic or disturbing behaviour.

In the case of schizophrenia it has been estimated that the cost to the economy of the USA in terms of provision of treatment and care, and loss of earnings, is in the order of $15 billion annually (Gunderson & Mosher, 1975). This is roughly 2 per cent of the gross national product, suggesting a cost of £2 billion – £3 billion per year in the UK. The availability of antipsychotic drugs means that many sufferers today can obtain significant relief from symptoms. Unfortunately these drugs do not provide a cure, and approximately two-thirds of cases experience recurring episodes of illness. Although there is increasing evidence that psychotic illnesses are associated with brain abnormalities, the precise causes remain unknown.

THE DEVELOPMENT OF THE PSYCHOTIC DIAGNOSES

The history of our current concepts of the psychoses is very firmly rooted in the work of Emil Kraepelin (1896) and Eugen Bleuler (1913). Kraepelin was the first clinician to divide the huge and diverse concept that was "insanity" or "madness" into two major, distinct syndromes: "dementia praecox" and manic-depressive psychosis. He was steadfast in his belief that these were physical diseases like any other, and he distinguished the two disorders on the grounds of differential patterns of course and outcome. "Dementia praecox", he suggested, almost invariably resulted in a global deterioration of the patient's mental state: from dementia praecox there was no reprieve. Manic-depressive psychosis, on the other hand, was characterized by a remitting course, with the patient experiencing a restitution of function between psychotic episodes.

Bleuler, for his part, coined the term "schizophrenia" (from the Greek *schizein*, to split, and *phren*, mind) to describe not a "Jekyll and Hyde" syndrome as is the common misconception of the disorder, but a condition

24

that took the form of a splitting up of different psychological faculties, such as emotion and language. Not surprisingly, when these conceptions were used as the basis of diagnosis, much confusion ensued. For a period during the 1950s and 1960s, diagnostic practices in Europe (where the Kraepelinian view prevailed) and the USA (where Bleulerian symptoms provided the focus) were markedly different. This situation has been greatly improved since the early 1980s with psychologists and psychiatrists around the world recognizing the need for greater cooperation and standardization in diagnostic procedures.

The two main classification systems in use today are the *International Classification of Diseases* (ICD-9) (World Health Organization, 1978) and the American Psychiatric Association's *Diagnostic and Statistical Manual of Mental Disorders* (DSM-IIIR) (American Psychiatric Association, 1987) – see Table 1. These diagnostic schemes are continuously under review and revised versions appear from time to time. Because we have no objective or biological marker for psychotic disorders, these diagnostic systems are largely based on the abnormal experiences and beliefs reported by the patient.

Paranoid psychosis can be seen as a variant of schizophrenia. In DSM-IIIR, Delusional (Paranoid) Disorder is diagnosed when patients have circumscribed, plausible delusions (for example, that they are being followed, or that their spouses are deceiving them), in the absence of bizarre behaviour or experiences.

Generally speaking, the diagnosis of affective psychosis is applied when a patient reports psychotic symptoms (that is, hallucinations and/or delusions)

Table 1 Summary of DSM-IIIR criteria for a diagnosis of schizophrenia

The patient must have

A   Characteristic psychotic symptoms for at least one week
B   Marked deterioration of functioning in self-care, work, or social relations
C   No major changes in mood (depression or elation)
D   Continuous signs of disturbance for at least six months
E   No evidence of organic factors (e.g., drug abuse)

Characteristic psychotic symptoms must include

1   two of the following:

(a) delusions
(b) prominent hallucinations
(c) incoherence or marked loosening of associations
(d) catatonic behaviour
(e) flat or grossly inappropriate affect

OR 2   bizarre delusions (e.g., thought broadcasting)
OR 3   prominent hallucinations of a voice

and also experiences pathological mood states (extreme elation or depression). Perris (1966) suggested that two distinct groups of these patients could be distinguished: those who suffer both manic and depressive episodes and those who experience *only* depressive psychosis. The terms *bipolar* and *unipolar* are often used to describe these two syndromes. There are also patients who meet DSM-IIIR criteria for schizophrenia and a major depressive or manic episode; these patients are classified as "schizo-affective".

PSYCHOTIC SIGNS AND SYMPTOMS

The experiences of persons in the grip of psychotic episodes recorded in centuries past are remarkably similar to the kinds of feelings and ideas described by sufferers today. Consider the extracts below. The first is from *The Life of the Reverend Mr George Trosse*, an autobiographical account of psychotic illness published in 1714. The second is from a letter written by a young man experiencing his first psychotic episode in 1992.

> Every person I saw seem'd to me to be an Executioner; and I thought every Thing either an instrument of, or a Preparation for, my Misery and Torture. I apprehended Self-Murther to be the only wise and charitable Act that I could do for my self, as the only Prevention of all expected and dreaded Torment. (Quoted in Peterson, 1982, p. 37)

> This ward is not a real one.... It is made up of black magic people.... It's horrific... I am to be eliminated soon.... Can you suggest a means of suicide?

The content, that is, the actual circumstance or subject referred to, is different, but the *form*, the way in which that content is processed or interpreted, is similar in both. The same process is reflected in the expression of symptoms in different cultures: whereas a patient in the Middle East may believe he is the direct descendant of the prophet Muhammad, his counterpart in Ireland might consider himself the new risen Christ.

Such ideas or beliefs would be classified as delusions – by far the most common of the psychotic symptoms. Jasper (1962) wrote: "Since time immemorial, delusion has been taken as the basic characteristic of madness. To be mad was to be deluded" (p. 93).

Delusions

Delusions may present as part of a complex of psychotic phenomena as in schizophrenia, mania, or psychotic depression, or as the lone, predominant psychotic feature of a paranoid psychosis. They may also occur in "organic" brain states, such as epilepsy. Jasper defined a "primary delusion" as follows: (1) it is held with extraordinary conviction, (2) it is impervious to other experiences and to compelling counter-argument, and (3) the content is incompatible with reality. Delusions are not, therefore, fleeting ideas; they are persistent, and they are experienced as true by the patient. Indeed, patients may be so convinced of the truth of their delusions that they will act on the basis of their content.

Curiously, certain themes appear to have an affinity for the delusional form. The belief that one is being persecuted by other people, watched by other people, the subject of some hateful plot, is the essence of what is perhaps the most common delusion – the delusion of persecution. Intimate relationships also feature in delusional content as in delusional or morbid jealousy, and the de Clerambault delusion, wherein the subject, typically a woman, believes a man with whom she has little or no real contact is actually her lover or husband. One such case known to the authors insisted that she had not actually married her real husband, writing to various registry offices making appointments to marry her "true lover". Delusions may, however, cover any topic, and they can be frankly bizarre: one patient informed us that "my friend Frank was actually Einstein in a previous life". Some patients present with one preoccupying delusion, while others may have a number of delusions which may be organised to greater or lesser degrees into a unified system of explanation (for example, "I am the son of God"; "I was born of a virgin mother"; "I have a special mission on earth the details of which God will communicate to me when the time comes").

Delusions can simply come "out of the blue": the patient will argue that he or she "just knew". In other cases they may rise out of a period during which the person feels the world, or the immediate surroundings, or people, have changed in some subtle, not obviously perceptible way; there is a feeling that something peculiar or sinister is going on and the patient, not surprisingly, may feel perplexed or anxious. This state is referred to as "delusional mood" or "delusional atmosphere". This period may last for days or weeks and almost invariably gives way to the formation of concrete, fully formed delusions, a process which usually has the effect of providing a release from the preceding state of tension. Once formed, delusions are likely to stay with the patient for a considerable time.

The delusions associated with the affective psychoses tend to have contents that are congruent with the mood of the patient. In a manic phase the patient will believe that he or she has superhuman abilities and is related to royalty, while when depressed he or she will feel responsible for all the troubles of the world.

Passivity experiences

Delusions, as pathological beliefs, obviously represent a disorder in the content of thought. However, a less apparent aspect of their character is the fact that they are also experienced, in the sense that one "feels" one knows something. At present we do not know whether or not a pathological process in this latter domain contributes to the formation or maintenance of delusions.

Certainly, abnormal "feelings" (by which we mean sensations) abound in the psychotic disorders.

In what is termed a "passivity phenomenon", patients report that their actions are not of their own doing but are in fact the actions of some other force which takes over control of their movements. Similarly patients will say that their thoughts are not their own but actually the thoughts of some external agency; again this is based on direct experience – the thoughts in my head do not feel like they are my thoughts. The opposite also occurs with patients reporting that they feel thoughts being physically withdrawn or "plucked" from their head. Because patients describe these experiences in terms of external forces or agencies, they have been called "delusions of control". However, what patients are describing here is an experience of their behaviour not being – or not feeling – generated, initiated, or maintained by themselves. In eliciting symptoms from a patient one must take great care to ascertain whether what the patient is reporting is simply a belief (for example, that people can put thoughts into other people's heads), or a belief based on an experience or sensation. Such experiences occur predominantly in schizophrenia (Schneider, 1959), but they can also occasionally be observed in manic patients.

Hallucinations

Among the most distressing of psychotic experiences are auditory hallucinations, that is, sounds, music, or "voices" experienced in the absence of an external stimulus. "Voices" coming through the ears (true hallucinations) or from inside the head (pseudo-hallucinations) are the most commonly experienced form. Those who experience such hallucinations think they are "real"; they are not, as far as the patients are concerned, imaginary. They may be unlikely, they may be odd, but they exist.

"Voices" may be male or female or "distorted". Some patients will identify them as the voices of individuals known or related to them. They are frequently interpreted in a manner consistent with concurrent delusions, so that the voice is construed as the voice of God or the devil, for instance. Typically, they enter the patients' consciousness in brief bursts over a period of time; in severe cases, however, they may be virtually continuous. The kinds of things that the voices say range from single words (for example, "go", "dirt") to complete sentences (for example, "You are unclean"). Schneider (1959) identified three distinct types of voices which he suggested are strongly associated with schizophrenia in particular: (1) two or more voices discussing the subject in the third person (e.g., "He is dishonest"); (2) voices commenting on the person or their actions (e.g., "He's opening the door now"); (3) voices repeating or anticipating the subject's own thoughts.

Occasionally, patients say they can have conversations with these voices; however, what they seem to be describing here takes the form of a "voice" commenting on events, to which the patient answers back, followed by another comment from the voice to which the patient again replies; this "conversation" does not have the quality of exchange of information that is usual in normal conversations.

While some patients say they can "ignore" the voices, many find their content and tone, which can be derogatory, accusatory, or obscene, very disturbing. Relentless voices of this kind, and those that instruct or demand the patient to commit acts that are unconscionable, reduce some patients to states of nothing less than torture and torment. During a psychotic depression, for example, patients may report hearing voices saying that they are worthless and should kill themselves.

Though much less common, hallucinations also occur in other sensory modalities: patients may report "visions"; unusual smells in a room or emanating from their own body; or physical sensations, as if someone was touching them, or even trying to have sexual intercourse with them. Again, as in delusional states, patients may feel compelled to act on the basis of these psychotic experiences.

Delusions, passivity phenomena, and hallucinations are subjective experiences. They are psychotic symptoms which we can infer only on the basis of the patient's verbal report. Other symptoms of this kind include "thought broadcasting", where the patient reports the experience of thoughts not being confined within his or her own mind but somehow managing to become available to others in their minds. There is also "thought echo" – the experience of one's thoughts being repeated or echoed inside one's head.

Thought disorder

While we can know about delusions and hallucinations only because the patient tells us about them, other psychotic symptoms are directly observable. The most dramatic of these is "formal thought disorder", a complex and ill-understood phenomenon whose defining characteristic is that the speech output of the patient is, in the severest case, almost entirely incomprehensible. This lack of comprehensibility can arise as a result of various combinations of abnormalities in the patient's attempts at communication. Andreasen (1979) has produced a scale for the assessment of these various abnormal features which include: derailment (that is, a lack of proper connection between phrases or ideas); incoherence (a lack of proper connection between words; loss of goal; failure to follow a chain of thought through to its natural conclusion); and tangentiality (oblique or irrelevant replies). The speech of patients with this symptom may also be dotted with neologisms (nonsense words, for example, "fancitung", "frowen") or clang associations (for example, "all the usual blah, la di da"). It is important to note that patients exhibiting "formal thought disorder" as manifest in their verbal utterances are not impaired in their understanding of speech. They do

29

understand statements directed at them; their problem lies purely in the domain of producing an adequate and appropriate response to that statement. Manic patients may also show incoherent speech. In addition they may also show "pressure of speech" in which words are produced at an abnormally high rate.

Expression of emotion

In fact, formal thought disorder occurs relatively infrequently; much more common are observable abnormalities in the expression of emotion. Blunting, flattening, and incongruity of affect are frequently observed in schizophrenia. Blunting refers to an apparent lack of emotional sensitivity; events or situations do not elicit the usual, normal emotional response. Flattening of affect describes a more pervasive, general absence of emotional expression. The patients appear devoid of emotional tone, presenting with minimal inflection in their speech (even though they may be recounting the most bizarre or disturbing experiences), and a lack of the normal variation of facial or bodily movements which convey feelings or emotions. Incongruity of affect, by contrast, is observed when the patient expresses emotions that are at odds with the circumstances. Thus, a patient may smile as she describes how she found her brother dead.

Poverty of behaviour

Also noted in schizophrenia are "poverty of speech" and "poverty of content of speech". The former refers to an extremely low level of speech output, such that the patient provides minimal, often monosyllabic responses in communication. The latter refers to an excessively low level of information in a normal rate of output; the patient expresses him/herself in a vague and repetitive manner. In addition to poverty of speech, poverty of thought and poverty of action may also be observed, especially when the illness has reached a chronic stage. Poverty of speech and action can also be observed in affective psychoses, but in these cases it would be associated with severe depression.

AETIOLOGY OF THE PSYCHOSES

Historically, the question of the aetiology of the psychoses has proved to be something of a "battleground" for the forces of psychological and medical science. Influential psychological explanations have propounded the role of deviant family relationships and patterns of communication, or stress, while biologically oriented researchers have argued forcefully for genetic or viral causes. However, psychological and biological explanation are not necessarily mutually exclusive. Increasingly, investigators in this field are coming to accept that each may have a contribution to make to the understanding of the aetiology of these disorders.

Evidence for a biological component in the aetiology of these disorders can be drawn from two main sources: epidemiological and genetic studies.

Epidemiological studies

The World Health Organization's series of epidemiological studies of schizophrenia have generated a database of over 3,000 clinically and socially documented cases in centres spanning Africa, Asia, Europe, and the Americas. Most importantly, patients enrolled in the initial study have been followed up and reassessed two and five years later (see Leff, Sartorius, Jablensky, Korten, & Ernberg, 1992). The results of this major initiative are quite clear-cut. First, the psychopathological syndromes considered to be characteristic of schizophrenia are present in all cultures and geographical areas studied. Second, when a "conservative" definition of schizophrenia is applied, the incidence rates across cultures vary to a very small degree: 0.7 per 10,000 in Aarhus (Denmark) to 1.4 per 10,000 in Nottingham (UK). Third, although the total cumulative risk for developing schizophrenia is about equal for women and men, in all cultures investigated there is a well-established difference in the age of onset of the disease, with men typically experiencing their first episode in their early 20s, women in their late 20s to early 30s. Finally, all centres reported a similar relationship between "mode of onset", meaning the manner in which the disorder developed from the first sign of a psychotic illness into the complete syndrome, and the subsequent course of the illness. The degree of similarity both in the incidence and the characteristics of the illness across very different cultures and geographical areas is striking and provides strong evidence for biological causal mechanisms.

The genetics of psychotic disorders

It is widely accepted that schizophrenia and manic-depressive psychosis are in some part genetically determined. Family studies have demonstrated that the risk of developing schizophrenia rises with the degree of genetic proximity to an affected individual (see Table 2).

Data obtained from adoption and twin studies have further consolidated the genetic interpretation of the results of these family studies (Gottesman & Shields, 1982). The results of similar kinds of studies of affective disorder also point to a significant degree of genetic determination in bipolar or manic-depressive disorder (see McGuffin & Katz, 1986).

31

Table 2 Lifetime expectancy of schizophrenia in the relatives of schizophrenic patients

Relative	*% Schizophrenic*
Parent	5.6
Sibling	10.1
Children (one parent affected)	16.7
Children (both parents affected)	46.3
Uncles/aunts/nephews/nieces	2.8
Unrelated	0.86

Source: Data abstracted from Gottesman and Shields, 1982

Other risk factors

Compelling as these data are in respect of the genetic hypothesis of the aetiology of psychotic disorders, they fall far short of being able to explain all instances of these illnesses: many monozygotic twins (who are genetically identical) are discordant for the illness (that is, only one twin is affected); the majority of diagnosed cases do not report a family history; and the modes of inheritance (that is, the precise mechanisms by which the putative abnormal genes are passed on to the next generation) remain elusive. Indeed, many investigators in the field are now of the opinion that the data gathered to date are most satisfactorily explained by a "multifactorial" model of these disorders. This kind of model posits that a number of genes may be involved in producing a continuum of liability, or predisposition, to developing the disorder, which may in turn interact with environmental factors before the illness is manifest. Environmental factors such as birth injury and viral infections during pregnancy are claimed to increase the risk of developing schizophrenia, but these effects seem to be small.

Evidence for a psychological component in aetiology

In studies of the aetiology of psychotic disorders, the only evidence for a psychological component that has managed to withstand methodological criticism concerns stress. Steinberg and Durrell (1968), for example, showed that the rate of schizophrenic breakdown in US army recruits was significantly higher in their first month of service than at any time in the following two years. They suggested that the transition from civilian life to army life, a time when one might expect an increase in the experience of stress, contributed to the occurrence of the illnesses. Further support for the "precipitating" role of stress comes from the work of Brown and Birley (1968), who found that schizophrenic patients had experienced significantly more life-events than controls drawn from the same neighbourhood in the 12 weeks preceding the onset of their illness. It is also plausible that the deleterious effects of high expressed emotion in patients' relatives (see below, on course and prognosis) in relation to relapse in schizophrenic patients could be mediated via increases in the level of stress.

BRAIN ABNORMALITIES AND THE PSYCHOSES

The mental abnormalities that define the psychoses are so severe that it seems not unreasonable to expect that associated brain abnormalities would be found. At the time that Kraepelin was studying dementia praecox, the characteristic neuropathological changes associated with organic dementias such as General Paralysis of the Insane (due to syphilis) and Alzheimer's disease had just been discovered. He expected that similar markers would be found for the psychoses. Nevertheless, the considerable effort expended by neuropathologists in this search met with surprisingly little success. More recently the picture has started to change. While no characteristic neuropathology has yet been found, we now have very strong clues available which are being vigorously pursued.

Functional brain abnormalities: dopamine and schizophrenia

In the 1950s a new class of drugs, the neuroleptics, which had dramatic effects on many psychotic symptoms, was discovered (see below, on treatment). A great many placebo controlled trials have been carried out (Davis & Garver, 1978) showing that these drugs can reduce the severity of the positive features of psychosis (hallucinations, delusions, thought disorder). It has also been shown that this therapeutic effectiveness depends on the extent to which the drug blocks dopamine receptors (Seeman, Lee, Chau-Wong, & Wong, 1976). Dopamine is a neurotransmitter. It is stored in certain neurons and is used to communicate between one neuron and another via dopamine receptors. Dopamine-blocking drugs prevent or reduce such communication. This observation among others lead to the dopamine theory of schizophrenia (Randrup & Munkvad, 1972). It was hypothesized that psychotic symptoms were associated with an excess of dopamine in the brain. More detailed observations suggest that this simple theory is not correct. Nevertheless it is clear that the dopamine system plays an important, though indirect, role in the production of psychotic symptoms. A great deal is known about the dopamine system. We know that dopamine-containing neurons are concentrated in the basal ganglia and in frontal cortex. These areas are concerned with the initiation and control of movement. Degeneration of the dopamine system is associated with Parkinson's disease. Sufferers from this disorder show a characteristic poverty of movement which bears a superficial resemblance to the motor retardation that can be observed in chronic schizophrenic patients and in patients with severe depression. These observations have important implications for developing a neuropsychology of psychosis (see, e.g., Robbins, 1990 and below, on mechanisms).

Structural brain abnormalities

The development of techniques for imaging the structure of the living brain has revolutionized the study of the psychoses. A large number of studies using these techniques have shown that the ventricles (the fluid spaces in the middle of the brain) are significantly enlarged in schizophrenic patients compared to controls (Gattaz, Kohlmeyer, & Gasser, 1991). This is by no means a change that is specific to the psychoses. Patients with degenerative brain disorders, such as Alzheimer's disease and Huntington's chorea, show considerably greater ventricular enlargement. Nevertheless, the result suggests that there is a lack of brain tissue in the psychoses, either because it has degenerated or because it failed to develop properly in the first place. Current opinion favours the hypothesis of developmental failure (e.g., Murray & Lewis, 1987). This is in part because there is no evidence that ventricle size increases with length of illness, and in part because there is little evidence for the gliosis (a kind of neural scar tissue) that is normally found in degenerative disorders. A number of investigations, particularly of post-mortem brains, have attempted to locate the missing and/or abnormal tissue. These results still remain somewhat inconclusive, but abnormalities of the medial temporal lobe in the region of the hippocampus have been reported in several independent studies (e.g., Brown et al., 1986).

MECHANISMS OF SIGNS AND SYMPTOMS

Psychotic patients have fundamental problems with behaviour, thought, and experience. Given that the brain serves to control behaviour and is the organ of thought, it is necessarily the case that these psychological abnormalities must be associated with parallel abnormalities of brain function. In principle, it should be possible to show that a particular symptom, such as an auditory hallucination, is associated with abnormal activity in a particular brain system. However, this does not mean that the hallucination is *caused* by this brain activity. Rather, the hallucination and the brain activity are two sides of the same coin. Likewise, the demonstration of relationships between symptoms and brain function does not mean that psychosis has a biological cause. Such demonstrations tell us nothing directly about aetiology.

Even if we had found specific neuropathological abnormalities in psychotic patients, we would still not understand why such patients heard non-existent voices or believed that alien forces were controlling their actions. In order to make a link between subjective experience and brain function we need a description of the relevant processes in cognitive terms.

Freud (1911) was probably the first to attempt an explanation of psychotic phenomena in terms of underlying cognitive processes, and Bleuler (1913) applied a similar approach to the study of schizophrenia. However, lacking the necessary methodology, these hypotheses were never tested experimentally. In this chapter we shall restrict our brief survey to accounts of psychotic signs and symptoms for which there is some empirical support.

Many different psychotic symptoms have been described, all of which could be studied separately. However, the very fact that these symptoms have all been classified as "psychotic" implies that they have something in common at the cognitive level of description. A number of studies have therefore searched for associations between signs and symptoms. The nature of the clusters revealed should tell us something about common underlying cognitive processes.

In studies of schizophrenia, the distinction made by Crow (1980) between positive and negative features has been particularly influential. Positive features are abnormal by their presence and include delusions, hallucinations, and incoherent speech. Negative features are abnormal through their absence and include poverty of speech, flattening of affect, and social withdrawal. Crow suggested that these two classes of symptoms were related to different pathological processes. Positive features are assumed to be associated with abnormal dopamine metabolism, and negative features with structural brain abnormalities. Subsequently, studies have been conducted which have refined Crow's description and have, with some consistency, revealed three clusters of features (Arndt, Alliger, & Andreasen, 1991). Liddle (1987) has named these "psycho-motor poverty" (poverty of speech, social withdrawal, flattening of affect), "disorganization" (incoherence of speech, incongruity of affect), and "reality distortion" (hallucinations, delusions). These clusters can also be observed in other types of psychoses. Psycho-motor poverty can be observed in depressed patients, and disorganization can be associated with mania. These three clusters provide a useful framework for considering the cognitive basis of psychotic features.

Poverty and disorganization

Typically patients with poverty of speech will answer questions put to them, but will use the minimum number of words with no spontaneous elaboration (see above, on signs and symptoms). Other areas of activity show the same pattern, in that patients respond appropriately in routine situations but produce no spontaneous activity of their own volition. These observations suggest a circumscribed deficit in the initiation of actions: spontaneous, "willed" actions are impaired, while routine actions elicited by appropriate circumstances (stimulus-driven acts) are not. Kraepelin (1896), in his original account of dementia praecox, concluded that this disorder was associated with a fundamental deficit of volition. Performance of patients with negative features on various experimental tasks are consistent with this hypothesis (Frith, 1992, chap. 4).

Shallice's Supervisory Attentional System (SAS) is a mechanism which can control the choice of actions in novel as well as routine situations and can account for the production of willed acts (Shallice, 1988, chap. 14). When this system is damaged, disorganization as well as poverty of action can occur, and thus impairments to such a mechanism could account for two different aspects of psychotic behaviour. Shallice's model was developed to explain abnormal behaviour after injury to the frontal lobes. A number of studies have shown that schizophrenic patients, particularly those with negative features, perform badly on "frontal lobe" tests, especially the Wisconsin Card Sorting Test (Corcoran & Frith, 1993).

This distinction between willed action and stimulus-driven action has also been made on the basis of neuro-physiological studies (for example, Goldberg, 1985). Goldberg has proposed that there is a motor system located in the medial part of the brain (including the prefrontal cortex, supplementary motor area, and the striatum) which is particularly concerned with the control of willed actions. He notes observations that patients with Parkinson's disease have much greater problems with willed acts than with stimulus-driven acts. On the basis of all these considerations, a number of authors have suggested that the negative features of schizophrenia are associated with abnormalities in a functional loop linking the frontal cortex and the striatum. This system is concerned with high-level control of action (for example, Robbins, 1990).

Reality distortion (hallucinations and delusions)

These phenomena are particularly difficult to study experimentally because they concern abnormal experiences which cannot be directly observed. Nevertheless, a number of accounts that are amenable to experimental investigation have been put forward.

Defective filter

One of the earliest insights of cognitive psychology was that we are all bombarded with a vast amount of information. A complex filtering mechanism ensures that most of this information remains in the "cognitive unconscious". Many positive features of psychosis can be explained as resulting from a breakdown in this filter (see e.g., Frith, 1979). For example, the patient becomes aware of irrelevant aspects of words such as their sound or alternative meanings. Such preoccupations can lead to incoherent speech, for example, a patient describing a light shade of green said, "Clean green. The one without the cream. Don't see this colour on planes. Looks like moss, boss" (Cohen, 1978). Likewise, patients who become aware of irrelevant stimuli in the environment may assume that these must be important and then develop complex delusional accounts as to why these stimuli are important to them. On this theory, delusions (false beliefs) are explained as occurring when normal logical arguments are applied to abnormal perceptions.

Gray and his colleagues (Gray, Feldon, Rawlins, Hemsley, & Smith, 1990) have put forward a detailed theory linking these kinds of psychological problems with impairments of a distributed brain mechanism involving the hippocampus and the dopamine system.

Self-monitoring

As yet there is no proven account of the mechanisms underlying auditory hallucinations. Currently, a popular notion is that auditory hallucinations are associated with the patient's own subvocal or "inner" speech. A few case studies have found hallucinating patients who were producing subvocal speech with the same content as their hallucinations (Gould, 1949). These observations imply that the hallucinating patient experiences his or her own inner speech or thought as alien and coming from some external source. This is an attractive idea since it could account for certain delusions (for example, the belief that my actions are being controlled by alien forces) as well as auditory hallucinations. Such delusions could arise if patients were unable to monitor their own intended actions and thus found themselves performing actions without being aware of any prior intention to do so. It is possible to study experimentally the ability to monitor our own actions, and there is some preliminary evidence that this ability is impaired in psychotic patients with delusions of alien control (Frith, 1992, chap. 5; Fritz & Done, 1989).

A simple physiological system which permits self-monitoring has been described in relation to eye movements and limb movements (Gallistel, 1980). Physiological studies that may have direct relevance to auditory hallucinations have shown that there are cells in the temporal cortex of the squirrel monkey that respond to vocalizations of other monkeys, but not to self-generated calls (Ploog, 1979). Defects in such a system could result in the monkey perceiving its own calls as emanating from another monkey and hence experiencing auditory hallucinations.

Abnormal inferences

Some researchers have suggested that delusions arise because processes of logic and inference are faulty (Garety, Hemsley, & Wesseley, 1991). There is some evidence that deluded patients reach conclusions on an abnormally small amount of evidence and then stick to these conclusions in the face of contradictory evidence. A major problem with this hypothesis is that most patients have circumscribed delusions. For example, the patient may believe that a small group of people is persecuting him or her. Application of logic to the behaviour of other people would be perfectly normal as would reasoning in other spheres. These observations suggest that there is no general problem with making inferences. One proposal is that certain psychotic patients have a specific problem with making inferences about the beliefs and intentions of other people (Frith, 1992, chap. 7). Studies of autistic children have shown that the ability to make inferences about the mental states of other people can be specifically impaired while other abilities remain intact. A failure in this "mind reading" module could explain certain psychotic features. Paranoid delusions occur when patients falsely infer that others intend to do them harm. Delusions of reference occur when patients falsely infer that others intend to communicate with them.

As yet there are no physiological data concerning how the brain represents mental states. However, there are studies suggesting that there are circumscribed brain systems concerned with social interactions. The orbital frontal cortex and temporal cortex have been implicated in these systems (Brothers, 1990).

COURSE, PROGNOSIS, AND THERAPEUTIC INTERVENTIONS

At the time of Kraepelin and Bleuler the majority of psychotic patients became permanent invalids condemned to insanity, and hence an asylum, for life. Guttmann, Mayer-Gross, and Slater (1939) surveyed the outcome of 188 schizophrenic patients in the Maudsley Hospital during the 1930s and reported that although some 22 per cent made a complete recovery, over half remained more or less incapacitated by the disorder (some 80 per cent were still hospitalized at follow-up).

Schizophrenia

Research since the early 1960s indicates that this largely hopeless course for schizophrenia has been altered substantially. Johnstone (1991), for example, surveyed a cohort of some 530 schizophrenic patients discharged from psychiatric services over a period of ten years (1975–1985) and found that on average these patients spent only 13.7 of the 120 months between 1975 and 1985 in hospital; when contacted in 1990, less than 10 per cent of the patients were receiving continuing in-patient care. Symptoms such as hallucinations and incoherence were absent in the majority of cases, although 47.2 per cent were still found to have varying degrees of delusional belief. However, more than 90 per cent of patients were receiving medical and/or social support, and 45 per cent were still under the care of a psychiatrist.

This pattern of clinical and social outcomes reflects the advances and shortcomings inherent in current treatment regimes. While drugs such as chlorpromazine, the anti-psychotic properties of which were first demonstrated in the early 1950s, have had profound effects in terms of the alleviation of some of the most distressing symptoms, these compounds do not provide cures as such; they do not correct the abnormality (or abnormalities) causing the disorder. Consequently, to keep symptoms at bay, the majority of patients who experience psychotic episodes must continue to take medication. The "prophylactic" efficacy of continuous or "maintenance" medication has been demonstrated in numerous clinical trials. Goldberg, Schooler, Hogarty, and Roper (1977), for example, in a study of 400 newly discharged schizophrenic patients found that those receiving "maintenance" drug therapy had a relapse rate almost half that of those who received a placebo treatment (48 per cent compared to 80 per cent).

Relapse, however, is not a cut-and-dried issue, entirely dependent on drug treatment. A wide range of factors contribute to the possibility of the re-emergence of psychotic phenomena. Strauss and Carpenter (1977) demonstrated that outcome may be partially predicted from measures of the patients' pre-morbid (that is, prior to their becoming ill) level of functioning: those with a good pre-morbid level of functioning having a better outcome. Vaillant (1964) demonstrated that characteristics of the initial episode of illness, such as an acute onset, the occurrence of a stressful life-event or situation at the time of onset, and the lack of a family history of schizophrenia, also predicted a relatively good outcome. Social psychological research has shown that relapse may also be determined to some extent by the impact of life-events such as the death of a close relative or a change of accommodation (Brown & Birley, 1968) and by the patients' experience of highly emotionally strained relationships within the family (Vaughan & Leff, 1976).

These findings point to a role for psychological input in the prevention of relapse. Thus, Leff, Kuipers, Berkowitz, Everlein-Vreis, and Sturgeon (1982) reported that the introduction of a psychologically defined intervention consisting of giving information regarding the disorder (schizophrenia) to relatives, and conducting regular fortnightly group meetings with relatives and family therapy sessions, all designed to lower expressed emotion and face-to-face contact, resulted in a significantly lower relapse rate (50 per cent in those not receiving the package as against 9 per cent in those who were). In a similar vein, Falloon et al. (1985) have championed the cause of problem-oriented and behavioural therapy sessions in the prevention of relapse, reporting figures for their programme consistent with those of Leff et al. (1982). It should be stressed, however, that this programme has an adjunctive role; numerous clinical trials have demonstrated that psychological interventions alone make no impact on this disorder (Goldberg et al, 1977).

Unfortunately, despite the best efforts of clinicians, many schizophrenic patients are unable to resume "normal" levels of adult functioning. Johnstone (1991) found that at follow-up some 58 per cent of their cohort were unemployed, 60 per cent were single, and many lived alone. There is also a small minority of patients (approximately 7 per cent) for whom the drugs are of little benefit (e.g., Johnstone, 1991). For the majority it is still disappointing that the treatment regimes available provide varying degrees of control of positive symptoms but may have negligible impact on the negative symptoms. Thus, patients may not hear the voices as often as they used to, but they remain apathetic and withdrawn. There is the additional problem that anti-psychotic drugs have side-effects which not only are uncomfortable for the patient but also can compromise the patient's physical appearance (examples are weight gain, tremor, stiff gait). These problems, together with psychosocial factors, such as the strain imposed on relationships by the patient's behaviour during a psychotic episode, or the social stigma surrounding mental illness, preclude many from achieving stable or satisfying relationships or employment.

Affective psychoses

The outlook for patients suffering manic-depressive psychosis is not so bleak. As Kraepelin originally suggested, these patients typically make a good recovery from their psychotic episodes, although the episodes are likely to recur. Manic episodes of illness last approximately one to three months, whereas depressive episodes tend to be of longer duration generally, between three and eight months. The risk of recurrence of a manic episode is high, particularly if the person has his or her first episode before the age of 30. The time between bouts of illness is extremely variable, ranging from weeks to years.

Treatment of manic-depressive psychosis consists largely of drug therapies, the most appropriate form being determined by the current presentation. In depressive episodes patients are prescribed standard anti-depressive drug regimens, whereas patients in a manic state are likely to be treated initially with an anti-psychotic, following which lithium – a drug of unique value in the treatment of manic-depressive psychosis – may be introduced. The principal use of lithium is to prevent recurrence of mania and depressive episodes. How it achieves this is still unknown.

CONCLUSIONS

Psychotic disorders are associated with severe abnormalities in all the domains that reach their highest level of development in humans: emotion, will, consciousness, and the ability to interact with other minds. Currently the greatest challenge facing science is to explain how these mental entities can arise from a physical brain. Studies of psychotic illness will provide critical information for this endeavour. Such studies are also vital if we are to improve our ability to reduce the widespread suffering associated with these disorders.

FURTHER READING

Cutting, J. (1985). *The psychology of schizophrenia*. Edinburgh: Churchill Livingstone.

Frith, C. D. (1992). *The cognitive neuropsychology of schizophrenia*. Hove: Lawrence Erlbaum.

Gottesman, I. I., & Shields, J. (1982). *Schizophrenia: The epigenetic puzzle*. Cambridge: Cambridge University Press.

Sims, A. (1988). *Symptoms in the mind. An introduction to descriptive psychopathology*. London: Baillière Tindall.

Straube, E. R., & Oades, R. D. (1992). Schizophrenia: *Empirical research and findings*. London: Academic Press.

Wing, J. K., & Wing, L. (1982). *Handbook of psychiatry, vol. 3. Psychoses of uncertain aetiology*. Cambridge: Cambridge University Press.

REFERENCES

American Psychiatric Association (1987). *Diagnostic and statistical manual of mental disorders* (3rd edn, revised). Washington, DC: APA.

Andreasen, N. C. (1979). Thought, language and communication disorders. *Archives of General Psychiatry, 36*, 1315–1321.

Arndt, S., Alliger, R. J., & Andreasen, N. C. (1991). The distinction of positive and negative symptoms: The failure of a two-dimensional model. *British Journal of Psychiatry, 158*, 317–322.

Bleuler, E. (1913). *Dementia Praecox or the group of schizophrenias* (trans.). In J. Cutting & M. Shepherd (Eds) (1987). *The clinical routes of the schizophrenia concept* (pp. 59–74). Cambridge: Cambridge University Press.

Brothers, L. (1990). The social brain: A project for integrating primate behaviour and neurophysiology in a new domain. *Concepts in Neuroscience, 1*, 27–51.

Brown, G. W., & Birley, J. L. T. (1968). Crises and life changes and the onset of schizophrenia. *Journal of Health and Social Behaviour, 9*, 203–214.

Brown, R., Colter, N., Corsellis, J. A. N., Crow, T. J., Frith, C. D., Jagoe, R., Johnstone, E. C., & Marsh, L. (1986). Post-mortem evidence of structural brain changes in schizophrenia. *Archives of General Psychiatry, 43*, 36–42.

Cohen, B. D. (1978). Referent communication disturbances in schizophrenia. In S. Schwartz (Ed.) *Language and cognition in schizophrenia* (pp. 1–34). Hillsdale, NJ: Lawrence Erlbaum.

Corcoran, R., & Frith, C. D. (1993). Neuropsychology and neurophysiology of schizophrenia. *Current Opinion in Psychiatry, 6*, 74–79.

Crow, T. J. (1980). Molecular pathology of schizophrenia: More than one disease process? *British Medical Journal, 280*, 66–68.

Davis, J. M., & Garver, D. L. (1978). Neuroleptics: Clinical use in psychiatry. In L. L. Iversen & S. D. Iversen (Eds) *Handbook of psychopharmacology* (vol. 10, pp. 129–164). New York: Plenum.

Falloon, I. R. H., Boyd, J. L., McGill, C. W., Williamson, M., Razani, J., Moss, H. B., Gilderman, A. M., & Simpson, G. M. (1985). Family management in the prevention of morbidity of schizophrenia. *Archives of General Psychiatry, 42*, 887–896.

Freud, S. (1911). Psychoanalytic notes upon an autobiographical account of a case of paranoia (dementia paranoids). In S. Freud, *Collected papers* (J. Strachey, ed. and trans., vol. 3, pp. 387–470). London: Hogarth.

Frith, C. D. (1979). Consciousness, information processing and schizophrenia. *British Journal of Psychiatry*, *134*, 225–235.

Frith, C. D. (1992). *The cognitive neuropsychology of schizophrenia*. Hove: Lawrence Erlbaum.

Frith, C. D., & Done, D. J. (1989). Experiences of alien control in schizophrenia reflect a disorder in the central monitoring of action. *Psychological Medicine*, *19*, 359–363.

Gallistel, C. R. (1980). *Organization of action: A new synthesis*. New York: Lawrence Erlbaum.

Garety, P. A., Hemsley, D. R., & Wesseley, S. (1991). Reasoning in deluded and paranoid subjects: Biases in performance on a probabilistic inferencing task. *Journal of Nervous and Mental Disease*, *179*, 194–201.

Gattaz, W. F., Kohlmeyer, K., & Gasser, T. (1991). Computer tomographic studies in schizophrenia. In H. Hafner & W. F. Gattaz (Eds) *Search for the causes of schizophrenia* (vol. 2, pp. 242–256). Berlin: Springer.

Goldberg, G. (1985). Supplementary motor area structure and function: Review and hypotheses. *Behavioural and Brain Sciences*, *8*, 567–616.

Goldberg, S. C., Schooler, N. R., Hogarty, G. E., & Roper, M. (1977). Prediction of relapse in schizophrenic outpatients treated by drug and sociotherapy. *Archives of General Psychiatry*, *34*, 171–184.

Gottesman, I. I., & Shields, J. (1982). *Schizophrenia: The epigenetic puzzle*. Cambridge: Cambridge University Press.

Gould, L. N. (1949). Auditory hallucinations and subvocal speech. *Journal of Nervous and Mental Disease*, *109*, 418–427.

Gray, J., Feldon, J., Rawlins, J., Hemsley, D., & Smith, A. (1990). The neuropsychology of schizophrenia. *Behavioural and Brain Sciences*, *14*, 1–84.

Gunderson, J. G., & Mosher, L. R. (1975). The cost of schizophrenia. *American Journal of Psychiatry*, *132*, 901–906.

Guttmann, E., Mayer-Gross, W., & Slater, E. T. O. (1939). Short-distance prognosis of schizophrenia. *Journal of Neurology and Psychiatry*, *2*, 25–34.

Jaspers, K. (1962). *General psychopathology*. Manchester: Manchester University Press.

Johnstone, E. C. (Ed.) (1991). Disabilities and circumstances of schizophrenic patients: A follow-up study. *British Journal of Psychiatry*, *159*, suppl. 13.

Kraepelin, E. (1896) *Dementia Praecox* (trans.). In J. Cutting & M. Shepherd (Eds) (1987). *The clinical routes of the schizophrenia concept* (pp. 13–24). Cambridge: Cambridge University Press.

Leff, J., Kuipers, L., Berkowitz, R., Everlein-Vreis, R., & Sturgeon, D. A. (1982). A controlled trial of social intervention in the families of schizophrenic patients. *British Journal of Psychiatry*, *141*, 121–134.

Leff, J., Sartorius, N., Jablensky, A., Korten, A., & Ernberg, G. (1992). The international pilot study of schizophrenia: Five-year follow-up findings. *Psychological Medicine*, *22*, 131–145.

Liddle, P. F. (1987). The symptoms of chronic schizophrenia: A reexamination of the positive–negative dichotomy. *British Journal of Psychiatry*, *151*, 145–151.

McGuffin, P., & Katz, R. (1986). Nature, nurture and affective disorder. In J. F. W. Deakin (Ed.) *Biology of depression* (pp. 26–52). London: Gaskell and Royal College of Psychiatrists.

Murray, R. M., & Lewis, S. W. (1987). Is schizophrenia a developmental disorder? *British Medical Journal*, *295*, 681–682.

Perris, C. (1966). A study of bi-polar (manic-depressive) and unipolar recurrent depressive psychoses. *Acta Psychiatrica Scandinavica*, suppl. 194.

Peterson, D. (Ed.) (1982). *A mad people's history of madness*. Pittsburgh, PA: University of Pittsburgh Press.

Ploog, D. (1979). Phonation, emotion, cognition: With reference to the brain mechanisms involved. In G. Wolstenholme & M. O'Connor (Eds) *Brain and mind* (CIBA Foundation Symposium 69, pp. 79–98). Amsterdam: Elsevier/North-Holland.

Randrup, A., & Munkvad, I. (1972). Evidence indicating an association between schizophrenia and dopaminergic hyperactivity in the brain. *Orthomolecular Psychiatry*, *1*, 2–7.

Robbins, T. W. (1990). The case for a frontostriatal dysfunction in schizophrenia. *Schizophrenia Bulletin*, *16*, 391–402.

Schneider, K. (1959). *Clinical psychopathology*. New York: Grune & Stratton.

Seeman, P., Lee, T., Chau-Wong, M., & Wong, K. (1976). Antipsychotic drug doses and neuroleptic/dopamine receptors. *Nature* (London), *261*, 717–719.

Shallice, T. (1988). *From neuropsychology to mental structure*. Cambridge: Cambridge University Press.

Sims, A. (1988). *Symptoms in the mind. An introduction to descriptive psychopathology*. London: Baillière Tindall.

Steinberg, H. R., & Durrell, J. (1968). A stressful situation as a precipitant of schizophrenic symptoms: An epidemiological study. *British Journal of Psychiatry*, *114*, 1097–1105.

Strauss, J. S., & Carpenter, W. T. (1977). The prediction of outcome in schizophrenia: III. Five-year outcome and its predictors. *Archives of General Psychiatry*, *34*, 159–163.

Vaillant, G. E. (1964). Prospective prediction of schizophrenic remission. *Archives of General Psychiatry*, *11*, 509–518.

Vaughan, C. E., & Leff, J. P. (1976). Influence of family and social factors on the course of psychiatric illness. *British Journal of Psychiatry*, *129*, 125–138.

World Health Organization (1978). *Mental disorders: Glossary and guide to their classification in accordance with the ninth revision of the International Classification of Diseases*. Geneva: WHO.

3

INFANTILE AUTISM

Simon Baron-Cohen

University of London Institute of Psychiatry, England

Autism is often described as the most severe of all of the child psychiatric disorders. Why should this be? Surely each disability is severe in its own way? Autism has gained this reputation because, unlike all other childhood disorders, people with autism appear to be virtually cut off from other people – "in a world of their own". It is in this sense that autism is sometimes also categorized as a psychosis: like schizophrenia, autism appears to be qualitatively unlike anything in the normal range of experience. In contrast, neurotic disorders (such as anxiety or depression) seem closer to experiences in the normal range.

Even the other communication disorders of childhood do not leave the sufferer isolated to quite the same degree as occurs in autism. Thus, although dysphasic disorders of childhood include language comprehension or expression deficits, somehow the social contact between the sufferer and other people is not severed: children with various dysphasias still find some way of making and developing relationships with others. They may use sign-language, impoverished speech, or even simply eye-contact and gesture. This is not true of children with autism. For them, even understanding *what communication is for* seems to be missing. Why? As I shall describe, this is part of the *social* difficulties that lie at the core of autism.

WHAT IS AUTISM?

Autism is a psychiatric disorder which begins during the first three years of life (American Psychiatric Association, 1987). It affects approximately 4 children in every 10,000, although some studies have suggested it may be as common as 15–20 per 10,000 (Frith, 1989). Boys are affected three times as often as girls; two-thirds of children with the condition have learning difficulties in addition to the problems specific to autism. That is, two-thirds of children with autism have an IQ (or measured intelligence) below the average range (Rutter, 1985). Even those whose intelligence is in the normal range show an unusual pattern of skills, with visuo-spatial intelligence usually being superior to verbal abilities (Frith, 1989).

Various sets of diagnostic criteria exist (American Psychiatric Association, 1987; Rutter, 1985), but all of these share an emphasis on three key symptoms. First, the child fails to make normal social relationships, or to develop socially in the normal way. Instead, social interests tend to be one-sided, non-reciprocal, and exist only to satisfy the child's immediate wishes. Missing are any genuinely social games (or turn-taking), any attempt to share interests through *joint-attention behaviours* (such as using the pointing gesture to indicate things of interest to people, or showing people things of interest), normal use of eye-contact, or any friendship beyond the most superficial acquaintance. A lack of empathy is often identified as the central feature of the social deficit (Baron-Cohen, 1988; Hobson, 1986, 1993; Kanner, 1943).

Second, the child fails to develop language or communication in the normal way. This symptom can include a multitude of anomalies. For example, some children with autism are functionally completely mute, while others are slow learning to speak, and their language development severely limited. Yet others can speak in full sentences, but nevertheless show a range of speech abnormalities, and fail to use their speech appropriately to achieve communication or to use gesture in a normal way. These abnormalities are described in detail below.

The final symptom is repetitive behaviour, in conjunction with a lack of normal imagination. Thus, children with autism often carry out the same action over and over again, becoming quite distressed if other people attempt to prevent them from carrying out their repetitive rituals, and their play is often devoid of any apparent creativity or imagination (Baron-Cohen, 1987). During play, for example, children with autism often simply arrange objects in strict geometric patterns in the same way every day, rather than transforming objects into *pretend* or symbolic play, as normal children do even from the age of about 18 months (Leslie, 1987).

45

Tragically, while the symptoms may change in form as people with autism get older, and while with age a considerable amount of learning may be possible, autism appears to be a lifelong condition (Frith, 1989). Some claims of "cures" have been reported, but in none of these cases has recovery to a *normal* state been verified, and in the majority of cases individuals remain "odd" and obviously disabled in adulthood.

CAUSES

Various possible causes of autism have been identified, all biological, and all of these are assumed to disturb the normal development of the central nervous system (Gillberg, 1990). The major causes for which there is scientific evidence are genetic, perinatal, viral, and a variety of medical conditions.

The genetic evidence centres on the higher concordance rate for autism among monozygotic (genetically identical) twins, where one has autism, than among dizygotic (genetically non-identical) twins, where one has autism (Bolton & Rutter, 1990). In addition, some 2–3 per cent of the siblings of children with autism also develop autism, and this is approximately 50 times higher than one would expect from chance alone (Bolton & Rutter, 1990). The perinatal evidence centres on the increased risk for autism produced by a range of complications during pregnancy and labour. The viral evidence centres on the statistically significant association between autism and infection by the rubella (German measles) virus during pregnancy (Wing, 1969).

Finally, the range of medical conditions associated with autism (and assumed to be causal) include genetic disorders (such as Fragile X Syndrome, phenylketonuria, tuberous sclerosis, neurofibromatosis, and other chromosomal anomalies); metabolic disorders (such as histidinaemia, abnormalities of purine synthesis and of carbohydrate metabolism); and congenital anomaly syndromes (such as Cornelia de Lange Syndrome, Noonan Syndrome, Coffin-Siris Syndrome, Williams Syndrome, Biedl-Bardet Syndrome, Moebius' Syndrome, and Leber's Amaurosis). These are reviewed by Gillberg (1990).

No single cause has been identified for all cases, and current theories suggest that there may instead be several separate causes of autism, any of which may affect the part of the brain that produces the condition. This view has come to be known as the *final common pathway* hypothesis. Using neuro-imaging techniques, brain abnormalities have been found in various regions of the brain in different cases, but again none of these is consistent across all individuals with autism (George, Costa, Kouris, Ring, & Ell, 1993). The exception to this is the finding that the cerebellum may show specific atrophy in all cases (Courchesne, Yeung-Courchesne, Press, Hesselink, & Jernigan, 1988). This work remains to be replicated. But the clearest evidence that there is brain dysfunction in autism stems from the fact that some 30 per cent of people with autism also develop epilepsy at some stage in their lives (Rutter,

1985). Finally, autism has not been demonstrated to be associated with either poor parenting, or social factors such as class. This last statement rules out some early theories of autism. For example, Bettelheim (1968) had proposed that the mothers of children with autism gave inadequate emotional input to their children, preventing the formation of the primary bond between mother and child, and thus preventing further social development or development of the child's concept of self. Tinbergen and Tinbergen (1983) argued for a similar characterization of autism, emphasizing traumatic factors that might have prevented the primary mother–child attachment relationship from forming. Finally, Kanner (1943) emphasized the predominantly intellectual, upper-middle-class nature of the parents of children with autism, implying that a lack of emotion in the parents may have caused the child's autism. None of these claims has been supported by subsequent work (Frith, 1989).

WHAT ARE THE LANGUAGE ABNORMALITIES IN AUTISM?

Language abnormalities exist in all of the subsystems of language. In syntax, for example, there can be considerable delays in rate of acquisition of syntactical forms, although longitudinal studies show that the order of acquisition does not differ from that found either in normal children or in children with learning difficulties (Tager-Flusberg et al., 1990). Thus, children with autism who develop speech usually go through a one-word and a two-word phase, their *mean length of utterance* (MLU) usually increases in normal ways, and the syntactical forms used seem to appear in the same order as in normal development. In phonology, intonation can sometimes be rather monotonous and "mechanical" sounding, but otherwise is often normal, if not superior. Thus, when children with autism produce *echolalia*, echoing someone else's speech, it is often with identical intonation to the person who first uttered it.

In semantics, words are clearly referential, but neologisms may be present. Thus, the child may use a word that is not a conventional one, but which nevertheless has a meaning for that child. For example, one boy with autism referred to a cat as a "milk outside". When the origin of such neologisms is traced, they are often found to derive from incomplete learning during the first usage of the term. In the example above, the boy's mother often used to say "Let's put the milk outside for the cat". Kanner, the psychiatrist who first described autism in 1943, characterized such neologisms in the speech of children with autism as "metaphorical", although it is worth stressing that these do not conform to cases of true metaphor. Indeed, semantic abnormalities in the speech of people with autism include difficulties in understanding or creating true metaphors and other forms of figurative language, such as irony or sarcasm (Happé, 1992).

Other semantic abnormalities are seen in the production of echolalia – either *immediate*, where the person with autism repeats straight back what the other person has just said, or *delayed*, where the person repeats back a segment of conversation that was overheard some time before. In delayed echolalia, the speech echoed may be part of a television jingle, or lyrics from a song, and often testifies to excellent long-term memory in people with autism.

But of all the language abnormalities in autism, the most severe are in the pragmatics of speech. By pragmatics is meant the rules governing the appropriate *use* of language in specific social contexts, and the rules for inferring a speaker's intended meaning. Almost every aspect of pragmatics that has been studied in people with autism has been found to be abnormal (see Baron-Cohen, 1988, for a review). Thus, the range of *speech acts* that they produce is quite limited – requests being the most frequent, informative or humorous speech acts being quite rare. They also appear not to realize how to use language in a way that is sensitive to the social context. For example, they tend to say things that are rude, not because of any wilful desire to offend, but simply because they are blind to the polite/rude distinction (e.g., one child with autism correctly noticed but then said out loud "That woman has dyed her moustache!"). Furthermore, they often do not distinguish old and new information in a conversation, failing to take into account what the listener already knows or does not know. For example, they may repeat things they have already told the listener, or they may refer to things that the listener could not possibly know about, without explaining these. It is also rare for them to introduce their topic so that the listener can appreciate its relevance (e.g., by using phrases such as "You know I was in France for my holidays, well...").

Another instance of the pragmatic deficit in the language of people with autism is seen in the lack of normal turn-taking in conversation. Instead, they may talk at the same time as the other person, or deliver extended monologues, or simply not reply at all when a reply is expected. This can appear as a failure to recognize the intention behind a question. For example, when asked "Can you pass the salt?", a person with autism may simply reply "Yes". Such a limited reply is not a sign of wilful rudeness, but simply due to a failure to recognize the question as a request for an object.

The pragmatic deficit is also seen in the use of a pedantic style of language that is inappropriate for the social situation. For example, one girl with autism asked "Do you travel to work on a driver-only-operated number 68 bus?" Also, many people with autism do not establish eye contact with the listener before speaking, or use eye contact to regulate any conversational turn-taking. Finally, some studies have shown that they tend to ask questions to which they already know the answers, thus violating conventional uses of different parts of speech.

RELATIONSHIP BETWEEN THE LANGUAGE AND THE SOCIAL ABNORMALITIES

During the 1960s and early 1970s one major theory of autism argued that the social abnormalities in this disorder were secondary to the language problems (Rutter, 1985). This theory lost credibility when studies compared children with dysphasia and children with autism. Such studies demonstrated that language disabilities did not inevitably produce social disabilities, in that children with even severe dysphasia nevertheless often showed surprisingly intact social skills and sensitivities. In contrast, more recent psychological theories suggest that language delay is an entirely independent disability which may co-occur in autism, while the abnormalities in pragmatic competence are an inevitable consequence of the social disability in people with autism, and are seen in all cases. One such psychological theory is elaborated below.

THE MIND-BLINDNESS THEORY

Experiments have demonstrated that people with autism are severely impaired in their understanding of mental states, such as beliefs and thoughts, and in their appreciation of how mental states govern behaviour (Baron-Cohen, Leslie, & Frith, 1985; Baron-Cohen, 1993). This ability in normal people has been referred to as a "theory of mind" (Premack & Woodruff, 1978) because of how we use our concepts of people's mental states to explain their behaviour. Attributing mental states such as thoughts, desires, intentions, and so on to other people allows us to understand why people do what they do, and in keeping track of both other people's mental states and our own, we can mesh flexibly in social interaction.

Apart from using a theory of mind to make sense of the social world, and to participate in it (Dennett, 1978), a second key function of a theory of mind in normal people is to make sense of communication, and to communicate with others (Grice, 1975). In computing the meaning and relevance of another person's speech we constantly take into account their background mental states, and in making our speech meaningful and relevant to our listener, we do the same (Sperber & Wilson, 1986).

Given these two functions of a theory of mind, it is clear that, if people with autism are unable to appreciate that other people have different mental states, this would severely impair their ability not only to understand and participate in social interaction, but also communication itself. It is in this sense that the deficits they show in pragmatics are thought to be intimately entwined with their social deficits. A number of experiments have demonstrated specific difficulties for people with autism in understanding the mental states of belief, knowledge, pretence, and intention (Baron-Cohen et al., 1985; Leslie & Frith, 1988; Goodhart & Baron-Cohen, 1992; Phillips, 1993).

One example of a test of understanding belief is shown in Figure 1. This core inability to appreciate other people's mental states has been termed "mind-blindness" (Baron-Cohen, 1990). Current research is elucidating whether this problem constitutes a case of *specific developmental delay*, in that some children with autism do eventually develop a theory of mind, *years* after it emerges in normal development (Baron-Cohen, 1989a), and what the origins of their mind-blindness might be (Baron-Cohen, 1989b; Baron-Cohen, 1993; Hobson, 1993).

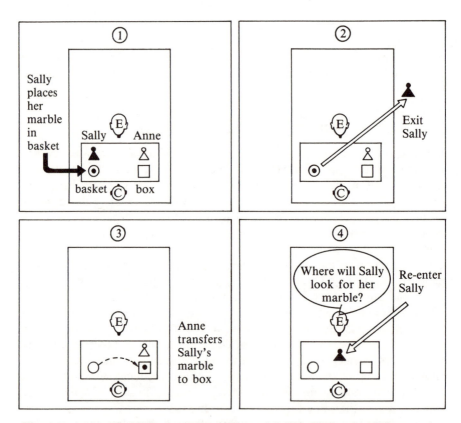

Figure 1 A test of children's understanding of belief. The story: *Sally puts her marble in the basket. Then she goes out. Anne takes Sally's marble, and puts it into her box. Then Sally comes back from her walk. Where will she look for her marble?* Normal 4-year-old children have no difficulty in correctly pointing to the basket, in answer to this question. In contrast, children with autism usually point (incorrectly) to the box

Source: Taken from Baron-Cohen, Leslie, and Frith, 1985, with permission

COGNITIVE MECHANISMS

The failure to develop a normal theory of mind in autism has been explained by several theories. Perhaps the most detailed account to date has been advanced by Leslie (1987; Leslie & Roth, 1993) who argues that in the normal case there is a specialized module called the *theory of mind mechanism* (ToMM) which matures around 12–18 months of age, and which processes information in the form of *metarepresentations*. These are essentially representations of mental representations, or representations of propositional attitudes. Leslie argues that this module for processing metarepresentations is not the same as a general capacity for representing *any* representation (such as a drawing, or a map, or a photograph). Rather, it is a highly specialized mechanism for representing *mental* representations. Evidence in favour of this specialized function comes from experiments showing that children with autism are able to represent non-mental representations such as photographs (Leekam & Perner, 1991) and drawings (Charman & Baron-Cohen, 1992), despite failing tasks of representing beliefs.

A second proposal, suggested by Frith (1989), is that the theory of mind deficit is just one part of a larger deficit in cognition, in the capacity for finding "central coherence": by this, she means the ability to use context to relate otherwise disparate sets of information. In the normal case, this ability to find central coherence can be seen in the non-social domain in our tendency to be distracted by overall *meaning* when perceiving a scene, rather than focusing on individual parts in the scene. Her work has shown that children with autism are more accurate in tasks such as the Children's Embedded Figures Test, in which the subject has to identify a target shape among a more complex, meaningful design (Shah & Frith, 1983), for example, identifying the triangle within the picture of the pram (depicted in Figure 2). By extension, she argues that in the social domain, theory of mind is par excellence an illustration of how we normally find central coherence. Rather than focusing on the myriad of individual behaviours, we focus on inferred mental states that we assume must underlie these behaviours. In Frith's theory, the superiority of children with autism on tasks like the Embedded Figures Test, and their deficits on theory of mind tasks, can be explained by reference to this single impairment in finding central coherence. Note that this explanation is opposed to Leslie's account, in that his account is highly modular, while hers is not. Frith's theory also predicts that children with autism should have difficulties in building *any* theory about some aspect of the world, not just a theory of mind. Tests of whether children with autism develop theories of biology would, for example, provide data with which to evaluate the coherence theory.

A third account that has been proposed is that the theory of mind deficits in autism may be secondary to deficits in *executive function* (Hughes, Russell and Robbins, 1993). By "executive function" is meant the ability to

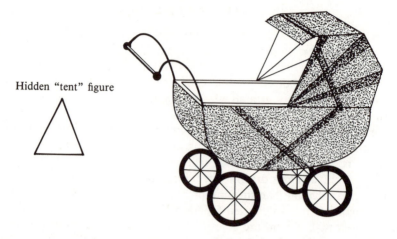

Hidden "tent" figure

Figure 2 An example of an item from the Children's Embedded Figures Test
Source: Described by Shah and Frith, 1983; reprinted with permission

inhibit responses to salient stimuli in the here-and-now, in favour of representations of objects, plans, or events that are not currently present. Individuals with autism, like many patients with frontal lobe damage, show impairments in tests of executive functioning (Hughes, Russell & Robbins, 1993; Ozonoff, Pennington, & Rogers, 1991), and this is the main evidence in favour of this account. An alternative possibility is that there is not a *single* cognitive deficit in autism, but rather there are several. It may be that the brain damage responsible for theory of mind impairments is localized in the same area of the brain that can also produce executive function deficits, namely, in the frontal lobe (Baron-Cohen et al., 1993). On this view, executive function and theory of mind deficits may be independent of one another, but tend to co-occur in the autistic syndrome by virtue of their neural proximity to each other. Testing the independence of these deficits is an important question for research in this area.

EARLY DIAGNOSIS

Leaving the question of the nature of the cognitive mechanism underlying the theory of mind deficit to one side, another area of research has been exploring developmental *precursors* to the theory of mind deficit in autism, partly towards understanding the ontogenesis of this psychological deficit, and partly to test if abnormalities in these precursors might be useful in the early diagnosis of autism. Candidate precursors of theory of mind are joint-attention skills (Baron-Cohen, 1989c, 1993) and pretend play (Leslie, 1987). Not only have these been found to be absent or impoverished in older children with autism (Baron-Cohen, 1987; Sigman, Mundy, Ungerer, & Sherman, 1986), but their absence in a sample of 18 month olds at raised genetic risk for autism predicted which children were undiagnosed infants with autism (Baron-Cohen, Allen, & Gillberg, 1992).

TREATMENT

Currently, treatment centres on special education for children with autism, and the most effective techniques seem to include highly structured, individually tailored behaviour therapy, aimed at skill-building, reducing difficult behaviours, and facilitation of educational achievements (Howlin & Rutter, 1987). Other specialist therapies also play important roles, and these include speech and music therapies. Sign-languages, such as Makaton or Paget-Gorman, are also used with some children with autism, if speech is particularly limited. However, none of these treatments claims any dramatic success in removing the core social abnormalities, although these may become less intrusive and disabling over time. Medical treatments exist for specific difficulties, such as epilepsy and hyperactivity, but at present there are no medical treatments which are useful in ameliorating the language or social difficulties in people with autism. Current and future research is aiming to find the links between the behavioural, psychological, and biological abnormalities in this condition, as well as aiming at developing more effective treatment and diagnostic methods.

ACKNOWLEDGEMENTS

This work was written while the author was in receipt of grants from the Medical Research Council, the British Council, the Royal Society, and the Mental Health Foundation. Parts of this chapter appeared in J. Cooper (Ed.) (1992). *The Encylopaedia of Language and Linguistics*. Oxford: Pergamon and Aberdeen University Press. Permission to reprint these parts is gratefully acknowledged.

FURTHER READING

Baron-Cohen, S., Tager-Flusberg, H., & Cohen, D. J. (Eds) (1993). *Understanding other minds: Perspectives from autism*. Oxford: Oxford University Press.
Frith, U. (1989). *Autism: Explaining the enigma*. Oxford: Basil Blackwell.
Howlin, P., & Rutter, M. (1987). *Treatment of autistic children*. Chichester: Wiley.
Schopler, E., & Mesibov, L. (1988). *Neurobiological issues in autism*. New York: Plenum.

REFERENCES

American Psychiatric Association (1987). *Diagnostic and statistical manual of mental disorders* (3rd edn). Washington, DC: APA.

Baron-Cohen, S. (1987). Autism and symbolic play. *British Journal of Developmental Psychology, 5*, 139–148.

Baron-Cohen, S. (1988). Social and pragmatic deficits in autism: Cognitive or affective? *Journal of Autism and Developmental Disorders, 18*, 379–402.

Baron-Cohen, S. (1989a). The autistic child's theory of mind: A case of specific developmental delay. *Journal of Child Psychology and Psychiatry, 30*, 285–298.

Baron-Cohen, S. (1989b). Are autistic children behaviourists? An examination of their mental–physical and appearance–reality distinctions. *Journal of Autism and Developmental Disorders, 19*, 579–600.

Baron-Cohen, S. (1989c). Perceptual role-taking and protodeclarative pointing in autism. *British Journal of Developmental Psychology, 7*, 113–127.

Baron-Cohen, S. (1990). Autism: A specific cognitive disorder of "mind-blindness". *International Review of Psychiatry, 2*, 79–88.

Baron-Cohen, S. (1993). From attention-goal psychology to belief-desire psychology: The development of a theory of mind and its dysfunction. In S. Baron-Cohen, H. Tager-Flusberg, & D. J. Cohen (Eds) *Understanding other minds: Perspectives from autism*. Oxford: Oxford University Press.

Baron-Cohen, S., Allen, J., & Gillberg, C. (1992). Can autism be detected at 18 months? The needle, the haystack, and the CHAT. *British Journal of Psychiatry, 161*, 839–843.

Baron-Cohen, S., Leslie, A.M., & Frith, U. (1985). Does the autistic child have a "theory of mind"? *Cognition, 21*, 37–46.

Baron-Cohen, S., Ring, H., Moriarty, J., Schmitz, B., Costa, D., & Ell, P. (1993). *The role of the orbito-frontal region of the brain*. Unpublished manuscript, Institute of Psychiatry, University of London.

Bettelheim, B. (1968). *The empty fortress*. Chicago: Free Press.

Bolton, P., & Rutter, M. (1990). Genetic influences in autism. *International Review of Psychiatry, 2*, 67–80.

Charman, T., & Baron-Cohen, S. (1992). Understanding beliefs and drawings: A further test of the metarepresentation theory of autism. *Journal of Child Psychology and Psychiatry, 33*, 1105–1112.

Courchesne, E., Yeung-Courchesne, R., Press, G., Hesselink, J., & Jernigan, T. (1988). Hypoplasia of cerebellar vernal lobules VI and VII in infantile autism. *New England Journal of Medicine, 318*, 1349–1354.

Dennett, D. (1978). *Brainstorms: Philosophical essays on mind and psychology*. Sussex: Harvester.

Frith, U. (1989). *Autism: Explaining the enigma*. Oxford: Basil Blackwell.

George, M., Costa, D., Kouris, K., Ring, H., & Ell, P. (1993). Cerebral blood flow abnormalities in adults with infantile autism. *Journal of Nervous and Mental Diseases*.

Gillberg, C. (1990). What is autism? *International Review of Psychiatry, 2*, 61–66.

Goodhart, F., & Baron-Cohen, S. (1992). *Do children with autism understand how knowledge is acquired?* Unpublished manuscript, Institute of Psychiatry, University of London.

Grice, H. P. (1975). Logic and conversation. In R. Cole & J. Morgan (Eds) *Syntax and semantics: Speech acts*. New York: Academic Press (original work published in 1967).

Happé, F. (1992). *A test of Relevance Theory: Communicative competence and theory of mind in autism.* Unpublished manuscript, MRC Cognitive Development Unit, London.

Hobson, R.P. (1986). The autistic child's appraisal of expressions of emotion. *Journal of Child Psychology and Psychiatry, 27,* 321–342.

Hobson, R. P. (1993). Understanding persons: The role of affect. In S. Baron-Cohen, H. Tager-Flusberg, & D. J. Cohen, (Eds) *Understanding other minds: Perspectives from autism.* Oxford: Oxford University Press.

Howlin, P., & Rutter, M. (1987). *Treatment of autistic children.* Chichester: Wiley.

Hughes, C., Russell, J., and Robbins, T. (1993). Autistic children's difficulty with mental disengagement from an object: Its implications for theories of autism. *Developmental Psychology.*

Kanner, L. (1943). Autistic disturbance of affective contact. *Nervous Child, 2,* 217–250. Reprinted in L. Kanner (1973). *Childhood psychosis: Initial studies and new insights.* New York: Wiley.

Leekam, S., & Perner, J. (1991). Does the autistic child have a metarepresentational deficit? *Cognition, 40,* 203–218.

Leslie, A. M., (1987). Pretence and representation: The origins of "theory of mind". *Psychological Review, 94,* 412–426.

Leslie, A. M., & Frith, U. (1988) Autistic children's understanding of seeing, knowing, and believing. *British Journal of Developmental Psychology, 6,* 315–324.

Leslie, A. M., & Roth, D. (1993). What autism teaches us about metarepresentation. In S. Baron-Cohen, H. Tager-Flusberg, & D. J. Cohen (Eds) *Understanding other minds: Perspectives from autism.* Oxford: Oxford University Press.

Ozonoff, S., Pennington, B., & Rogers, S. (1991). Executive function deficits in high-functioning autistic children: Relationship to theory of mind. *Journal of Child Psychology and Psychiatry, 32,* 1081–1106.

Phillips, W. (1992). *Comprehension of desires and intentions by children with autism.* Unpublished PhD thesis, Institute of Psychiatry, University of London.

Premack, D., & Woodruff, G. (1978). Does the chimpanzee have a "theory of mind"? *Behavioral and Brain Sciences, 4,* 515–526.

Rutter, M. (1985). Infantile autism and other pervasive developmental disorders. In M. Rutter & L. Hersov (Eds) *Child and adolescent psychiatry.* Oxford: Basil Blackwell.

Shah, A., & Frith, U. (1983). An islet of ability in autism: A research note. *Journal of Child Psychology and Psychiatry, 24,* 613–620.

Sigman, M., Mundy, P., Ungerer, J., & Sherman, T. (1986). Social interactions of autistic, mentally retarded, and normal children and their caregivers. *Journal of Child Psychology and Psychiatry, 27,* 647–656.

Sperber, D., & Wilson, D. (1986). *Relevance: Communication and cognition.* Oxford: Basil Blackwell.

Tager-Flusberg, H., Calkins, S., Nolin, T., Baumberger, T., Anderson, M., & Chadwick-Dias, A. (1990). A longitudinal study of language acquisition in autistic and Down's Syndrome children. *Journal of Autism and Developmental Disorders, 20,* 1–22.

Tinbergen, N., & Tinbergen, E. (1983). *Autistic children: New hope for a cure.* Oxford: Pergamon.

Wing, L. (1969). The handicaps of autistic children: A comparative study. *Journal of Child Psychology and Psychiatry, 10,* 1–40.

4

EATING DISORDERS

Peter J. Cooper
University of Cambridge, England

<table>
<tr><td>Diagnostic criteria</td><td>Physical factors</td></tr>
<tr><td>Epidemiology</td><td>Aetiology and maintenance</td></tr>
<tr><td>Clinical features</td><td>Treatment</td></tr>
<tr><td> Specific psychopathology</td><td>Course and outcome</td></tr>
<tr><td>   Eating habits</td><td>Further reading</td></tr>
<tr><td>   Beliefs and attitudes</td><td>References</td></tr>
<tr><td> General psychopathology</td><td></td></tr>
</table>

Accounts of self-induced weight loss can be traced back to the Middle Ages. However, the first clinical description of anorexia nervosa was provided in 1694 by an English physician, Richard Morton. He suggested the name *phthisis nervosa* for a disorder he had encountered in two of his patients involving food avoidance, extreme emaciation, amenorrhoea (cessation of menstrual periods), and overactivity. Morton regarded the disorder as neurological in origin, but recognized the influence of psychological factors. He reported that one of these patients, a "skeleton only clad with skin", died from "a multitude of cares and passions of the mind". The term *anorexia nervosa* was introduced into the medical literature in 1874 by Sir William Gull, Physician Extraordinary to Queen Victoria. Gull described a "peculiar form of disease" occurring mostly in young women, and characterized by extreme emaciation. He clearly regarded anorexia nervosa as essentially a psychological disorder. In 1914, the German pathologist Morris Simmonds reported a case of emaciation and amenorrhoea in a girl whose pituitary gland had atrophied. For the next 24 years most cases of anorexia nervosa were thought to be suffering from Simmonds' disease and were treated with pituitary extracts. Eventually it became clear that the pituitary disorder produces symptoms not found in anorexia nervosa and the two disorders were recognized as distinct. In the 1940s and 1950s theories of psychological causality flourished, the most influential early writer being Hilda Bruch (1973). Since then, there has been a remarkable consistency in the conceptualization of the disorder, with authorities in the field of varying theoretical orientations presenting accounts of the central psychopathological features in very similar terms (Crisp, 1967; Garfinkel & Garner, 1982; Russell, 1970).

Bulimia nervosa is a far newer clinical concept. Although there were a few early reports, it was towards the end of the 1970s that a number of clinical accounts began to emerge of people with a disorder characterized principally by episodes of uncontrolled eating. They closely resembled patients with anorexia nervosa in terms of their psychopathological features but were generally of normal weight. The disorder attracted a variety of names, but the two terms that gained widest acceptance were *bulimia nervosa* (Russell, 1979) and *bulimia* (American Psychiatric Association, 1980). The use of the term *bulimia* to refer to the disorder was unfortunate because it confused a behaviour (gross overeating) with a constellation of psychological characteristics in which bulimic episodes invariably occur. The revised version of the third edition of the American Psychiatric Association's (1987) *Diagnostic and Statistical Manual of Mental Disorders* (DSM-III-R) removed this ambiguity by adopting the term *bulimia nervosa*.

DIAGNOSTIC CRITERIA

Since Russell's (1970) seminal account of anorexia nervosa, there has been little disagreement about the necessary diagnostic criteria, which in itself is a testimony to the clarity with which the disorder presents itself. Table 1 shows the criteria proposed for the DSM-IV (American Psychiatric Association, 1991). Criterion A specifies a minimum degree of weight loss. This is presented in terms of a refusal to maintain a weight above 15 per cent below that expected (that is, for age, sex, and height). Criteria B and C specify the core psychological disturbance, sometimes referred to as the specific psychopathology of the disorder. The formulation of these criteria constitutes the first time any formal diagnostic system has explicitly included as a necessary criterion the notion of an overvalued idea about body shape and weight (embedded within Criterion C), although this has frequently been alluded to in the past in such terms as "a morbid fear of fatness" (Russell, 1970), "a pursuit of thinness" (Bruch, 1973), and a "weight phobia" (Crisp, 1967). The inclusion of amenorrhoea as a necessary condition (Criterion D) is intended to pick out the "secondary endocrine disorder" (Garfinkel & Garner, 1982). However, it is doubtful whether those who fulfil only Criteria A, B, and C differ in terms of their psychopathology from those who fulfil all four criteria. The proposed DSM-IV criteria include a "sub-typing" of anorexia nervosa into "bulimic type" and "non-bulimic type". This is

Table 1 Proposed criteria for DSM-IV for anorexia nervosa and bulimia nervosa

Anorexia nervosa

A Refusal to maintain body weight over a minimal normal weight for age and height (e.g., weight loss leading to maintenance of body weight 15% below that expected; or failure to make expected weight gain during period of growth, leading to body weight 15% below that expected).

B Intense fear of gaining weight or becoming fat, even though underweight.

C Disturbance in the way in which one's body weight or shape is experienced, undue influence of body shape and weight on self-evaluation, or denial of the seriousness of current low body weight.

D In females, absence of at least three consecutive menstrual cycles when otherwise expected to occur (primary or secondary amenorrhea). (A woman is considered to have amenorrhea if her periods occur only following hormone, e.g. oestrogen, administration.)

Specify type:

Bulimic type: During the episode of anorexia nervosa, the person engages recurrent episodes of binge eating.

Non-bulimic type: During the episode of anorexia nervosa, the person does not engage in recurrent episodes of binge eating.

Bulimia nervosa

A Recurrent episodes of binge eating. An episode of binge eating is characterized by both of the following:

   1 Eating, in a discrete period of time (e.g., within any two-hour period), an amount of food that is definitely larger than most people would eat during a similar period of time;

   2 A sense of lack of control over eating during the episode (e.g., a feeling that one cannot stop eating or control what or how much one is eating).

B Recurrent inappropriate compensatory behaviour in order to prevent weight gain, such as: self-induced vomiting; misuse of laxatives, diuretics or other medications; fasting; or excessive exercise.

C A minimum average of two binge-eating episodes a week for at least three months.

D Self-evaluation is unduly influenced by body shape and weight.

E The disturbance does not occur exclusively during episodes of anorexia nervosa.

Specify type:

Purging type: Regularly engages in self-induced vomiting or the use of laxatives or diuretics.

Non-purging type: Use of strict dieting, fasting, or vigorous exercise, but does not regularly engage in purging.

Source: American Psychiatric Association, 1991

sensible given the established differences between these two groups of patients in terms of a wide range of clinical features (Garfinkel, Modlofsky, & Garner, 1980).

The specification of diagnostic criteria for bulimia nervosa has generated rather more disagreement. The criteria proposed for DSM-IV (American Psychiatric Association, 1991), shown in Table 1, go a long way towards resolving earlier differences of opinion. Bulimic episodes, accepted by all previous criteria as a necessary condition, are clearly defined. Criterion B specifies the presence of one of a range of extreme or inappropriate measures to compensate for overeating or control weight. Criterion D (as was the case for Criterion C for anorexia nervosa) is an explicit recognition that a central feature of this disorder is an overvalued idea about shape and weight. Criterion C, the threshold criterion, is intended to exclude subclinical or partial cases. Criterion E, the exclusion criterion, is necessary because criteria A to D could be met by a patient fulfilling criteria for anorexia nervosa ("bulimic" sub-type). The proposed DSM-IV criteria include a sub-typing of bulimia nervosa into a "purging type" and a "non-purging type". This too is sensible given that most research into the disorder has been conducted on patients who purge and they may differ from those who do not purge but, say, fast is weak.

EPIDEMIOLOGY

Studies of the incidence and prevalence of anorexia nervosa are beset with methodological difficulties. Uncertainties concerning the definition of a "case", and the fact that many people with frank anorexia nervosa do not regard themselves as having a problem, make it difficult to derive accurate prevalence figures for anorexia nervosa from the community studies. Case register studies are difficult to interpret because they do not include mild cases that have escaped detection and because they are contaminated by the vicissitudes of diagnostic and referral practices. The latter point is well illustrated by a case-register study covering three distinct geographical areas: north-east Scotland, Munroe County in New York, and Camberwell in London (Kendell, Hall, Hailey, & Babigian, 1973). The estimates of incidence of anorexia nervosa varied from 0.37 per 100,000 per year in Munroe County to 1.6 per 100,000 per year in north-east Scotland. A consistent finding of the case-register studies is that there has been a sharp rise in the number of cases coming to specialist attention during the 1970s and 1980s. For example, Szmukler, McCance, McCrone, and Hunter (1986) reported that the rate of anorexia nervosa in north-east Scotland, based on records of contacts with the in-patient and out-patient psychiatric services, had risen from 1.60 per 100,000 per year for the period 1966 to 1969 to 4.06 per 100,000 per year for the period 1978 to 1982. A similar increase has been observed in the USA. It is likely that these well-documented changes in the number of cases being referred for treatment reflect a genuine increase in the incidence of the disorder. This conclusion is supported by a community-based epidemiological study in which the medical records of over 13,000 residents of Rochester (Minnesota) were examined for the period 1935 to 1984: over this 50-year timespan the age-adjusted incidence of anorexia nervosa among young women rose from 7.0 per 100,000 person years to 26.3 per 100,000 (Lucas, Beard, O'Fallon, & Kurland, 1991).

There have been several community studies of the prevalence of anorexia nervosa. In Britain, Crisp, Palmer, and Kalucy (1976) conducted a five-to-six-year retrospective survey of nine schools, seven private and two state run. Their estimate of prevalence was one case of anorexia nervosa per 100 girls aged over 16 in the private schools, and roughly one-fifth this rate among the girls in the state schools. A later survey has largely confirmed these findings (Mann et al., 1983). In this study the estimated prevalence of anorexia nervosa in six private schools was one case per 90 girls aged 16–18. A similar difference between state and private schools to that reported by Crisp and colleagues was found. A further finding of this study was that, among the girls in the private schools, in addition to the cases of anorexia nervosa, 5 per cent had sub-threshold disorders or "partial syndromes". A particularly notable prevalence study is that reported by Rastam, Gillberg, and Garton (1989), in that the total population of 15-year-old schoolchildren in Göteborg, Sweden, was screened using questionnaires, growth charts, and individual school nurse reports. After full clinical assessment and interviews with the mothers, 23 of the 4,291 children were found to have an eating disorder, and the prevalence of anorexia nervosa among the girls was 0.84 per cent. This figure must be regarded as an underestimate of the true rate in the community, given that girls over the age of 15 were not included in this survey.

Anorexia nervosa is a disorder that predominantly affects young women, only 5–10 per cent of cases being male. The most common ages of onset are 14 and 16, although cases with a considerably earlier onset do arise (Lask & Bryant-Waugh, 1992), as do some with an onset well into adult life. The disorder is over-represented in girls from upper socio-economic families. There is a striking elevation of prevalence of anorexia nervosa among those for whom a slim body shape has special significance, such as ballet and modelling students (Garfinkel & Garner, 1982). The disorder arises predominantly in western countries and developed non-western societies such as Japan. It is extremely rare in other cultures. The disorder also used to be rare among American blacks, but it appears to be increasing in this group (Hsu, 1990).

Little is known of the incidence of bulimia nervosa. The diagnostic concept is too new for case-register studies to be of use, and there have been no community studies that could cast light on the inception rate. Nevertheless, it is generally accepted that the incidence of the disorder has increased dramatically since the early 1980s. Although individual case histories can be found in the annals of psychiatry, and patients with 20–30-year histories are some-times seen, it was only towards the end of the 1970s that reports began to emerge of large numbers of these patients presenting for treatment.

There have been a number of attempts to estimate the prevalence of bulimia nervosa and its constituent components (Fairburn & Beglin, 1991). This work has produced conflicting findings, largely because of weaknesses in method. In particular, the great majority of the surveys have used simple self-report questionnaires with key concepts inadequately defined. Those studies that have used two-stage designs, with a clinical interview following a phase of screening by questionnaire, have been compromised by high attri-tion rates. Despite these difficulties, a consensus has emerged: among young adult women, bulimia nervosa appears to have a prevalence of 1–2 per cent (e.g., Cooper, Charnock, & Taylor, 1987; Schotte & Stunkard, 1987). Bulimia nervosa is largely confined to women; fewer than 5 per cent of cases presenting for treatment are men (Carlat & Camargo, 1991). The age of patients at presentation is somewhat older than those with anorexia nervosa, most being in their 20s, although a wide age range is affected. The social class distribution of patients has not been systematically studied, but it appears to be broader than that of patients with anorexia nervosa.

CLINICAL FEATURES

The clinical features of anorexia nervosa have been clearly described by numerous authorities in the field, such as Bruch (1973), Crisp (1967), Garfinkel and Garner (1982), and Russell (1970). There is wide agreement about the central features. More uncertainty has surrounded the core disturbance in bulimia nervosa. The clinical features of the eating disorders comprise features specific to these disorders and features more generally associated with psychological disturbance.

Specific psychopathology

Eating habits

Patients with anorexia nervosa markedly restrict their food intake. This involves a selective avoidance of food regarded as "fattening", generally leading to a high-protein low-carbohydrate diet. Frequently they monitor their calorie intake closely and set a rigid limit, usually in the region of 600–800 calories per day. The term "anorexia" is a misnomer because, except in long-standing cases, appetite for food persists. There is often an obses-sional component to these patients' eating habits: they may eat exactly the same food every day, cut up their food into very small pieces, or engage in other ritualistic practices surrounding eating. Associated with the efforts to restrict food intake there is a preoccupation with food and eating. Patients frequently spend hours poring over recipe books, cook elaborate meals for others, or choose jobs that involve working with food.

About half of those with anorexia nervosa alternate between episodes of dietary restriction and bulimic episodes. During such bulimic episodes food that is normally avoided tends to be consumed, sometimes in large quantities. The episodes lead to considerable distress and are a source of profound guilt and shame. Usually bulimic episodes are followed by self-induced vomiting. A number of consistent differences have been found between the bulimic and the restricting subgroups of patients with anorexia nervosa as regards presenting symptoms and history (Garfinkel, Modlofsky, & Garner, 1980). Patients with anorexia nervosa engage in a variety of weight control measures in addition to dietary restriction. Many induce vomiting, some abuse laxatives, diuretics, and appetite suppressants, and many exercise vigorously.

The principal complaint of patients with bulimia nervosa is that they have lost control of their eating. Thus they report episodes of gross overeating that are experienced as outside of voluntary control. The frequency of bulimic episodes varies between patients, but in one patient series, at presentation, half the patients reported that such episodes were occurring at least daily (Fairburn & Cooper, 1984). It is not unusual to see patients who are experiencing bulimic episodes many times a day. The proportion of protein, fat, and carbohydrate consumed in a bulimic episode is typically the same as that consumed by people with normal eating habits during an ordinary evening meal (Walsh, Kissileff, Cassidy, & Danzic, 1989).

Bulimic episodes are fairly uniform in nature. They are invariably secret, and food is usually eaten quickly with little attention being paid to its taste. They tend to consist of those foods that patients are at other times attempting to exclude from their diet. Typically, patients alternate between bulimic episodes and attempts to maintain a rigid diet. Strict dieting may be disrupted by dysphoric mood states and boredom, and by the belief that some dietary rule has been transgressed.

The body weight of patients with bulimia nervosa is usually within the normal range, reflecting a balance between the episodes of overeating and various compensatory behaviours designed to counteract the effects of bulimic episodes. The most common method of weight control is self-induced vomiting, which frequently terminates bulimic episodes. Vomiting is generally accomplished by inducing the gag reflex with the fingers, but around a quarter of these patients learn to vomit spontaneously. Vomiting is a source of considerable guilt and self-disgust and is almost always practised secretly. It may go undetected for many years. Self-induced vomiting is habit-forming. While it relieves the abdominal discomfort that results from overeating and lessens the risk of weight gain, it also appears to encourage overeating and therefore further vomiting. Purgatives are also used by some patients to control their weight. Like vomiting, purgative use can become habit-forming and, since tolerance develops, some patients increase their consumption progressively. As in anorexia nervosa, a variety of other methods of weight control are also practised by some patients.

Beliefs and attitudes

A central feature of the eating disorders is certain overvalued ideas concerning the importance of shape and weight. Thus, patients with anorexia nervosa place an abnormal degree of significance on the pursuit of a thin body shape, and they have an exaggerated fear of weight gain. Accompanying these extreme concerns, there is often a complete denial that they have any problems. Since Bruch (1973) first declared that a disturbance of body image was pathognomonic in anorexia nervosa, there has been a considerable amount of empirical work concerned with establishing whether patients with eating disorders overestimate their body size (Garfinkel & Garner, 1982). Two main methods of assessment have been used: the movable calliper technique, which provides data on particular body regions; and an image distorting technique, which provides data on patients' perception of their whole body. Using both techniques, as a group patients have usually been found to overestimate their body size, and in most studies this overestimation has been greater than that found in controls. However, many patients have been found to be accurate in their estimation of their body size and some have been found to underestimate their size. Moreover, many people with no eating disorder have been found to overestimate their size. Marked overestimation in patients has been found to be rare.

Patients with bulimia nervosa display similar concerns about their shape and weight to those with anorexia nervosa. In patients with bulimia nervosa the discrepancy between their actual body weight and desired weight is generally no greater than among normal young women; however, the discrepancy between their estimation of their body size and their desired size is substantial and significantly greater than among a control population (Cooper & Taylor, 1988). Thus, they tend both to overestimate their body size significantly more than do controls, and to have a desired size significantly smaller than that of controls.

General psychopathology

General neurotic symptoms are common in anorexia nervosa. Depressive symptoms are particularly prominent, with the level of depression positively associated with the degree of disturbance in eating habits and attitudes. Other symptoms present in anorexia nervosa are lability of mood, obsessional symptoms, and anxiety symptoms related to situations that involve eating. In more chronic cases hopelessness and suicidal ideation are sometimes present. Suicide is the most likely cause of death among those who die prematurely because of the disorder (Hsu, 1990).

The nature, frequency, and severity of the neurotic symptoms occurring in patients with bulimia nervosa has been systematically studied (Cooper & Fairburn, 1986; Fairburn & Cooper, 1984). A wide range of symptoms occur. Depressive and anxiety symptoms are particularly common. Studies in which the psychopathological profile of patients with bulimia nervosa have been compared with depressed and anxious patients (Cooper & Fairburn, 1986; Steere, Butler, & Cooper, 1990) reveal differences of clear diagnostic significance: the affective symptoms are predominantly secondary to the core eating disturbance in the patients with bulimia nervosa who present with more anxiety symptoms than depressed patients and more depressive symptoms than anxious patients.

Physical factors

One of the most striking features of anorexia nervosa is these patients' state of semi-starvation. This emaciation has wide-ranging effects on patients' physiology and also on their physical health (Mitchell, 1986a). Low body temperature, low blood pressure, and rapid heartbeat are common, as is lanugo hair on the back and face. Amenorrhoea is a *sine qua non*, arising from the low levels of gonadotrophins and gonadal steroids. Some patients have raised carotene and cholesterol levels. Starvation carries a marked risk of numerous complications including osteoporosis (reduction or atrophy of bone matter), liver function abnormalities, a low white blood cell count and a low platelet count, and impaired cardiac function. Some of the consequences of the emaciation interact with the central psychological disturbances. For example, slow gastric emptying, arising from low weight and reduced caloric consumption, leads patients to complain of fullness, bloating, and abdominal pain; and these symptoms are taken by them as evidence of the need for further dietary restriction. It has been argued that many aspects of the psychopathology of anorexia nervosa could be a direct result of starvation (Garner, Rockert, Olmsted, Johnson, & Coscina, 1985).

There are a number of physiological abnormalities and medical complications in bulimia nervosa (Mitchell, 1986b). Unlike anorexia nervosa, where most of these disturbances are the result of emaciation, most of those seen in bulimia nervosa result from specific behaviours, such as vomiting, purgative abuse, and the bulimic episodes themselves. Thus, the vomiting often leads to erosion of dental enamel and can lead to damage of the oesophageal sphincter; bulimic episodes frequently cause swelling of the parotid glands and, rarely, lead to acute dilation of the stomach. Complications associated with laxative abuse include profound constipation on laxative withdrawal and, in rare cases, permanent impairment of colonic function. Gastro-intestinal bleeding, malabsorption, and protein-losing gastric problems have also been described. Electrolyte abnormalities are common in these patients, the most significant being low potassium levels. Most of these physical disturbances are reversed by the restoration of normal eating habits.

AETIOLOGY AND MAINTENANCE

While the aetiology of the eating disorders is not known, it is widely accepted that a combination of biological, psychological, and social factors are of importance (Garfinkel & Garner, 1982). There has been a considerable amount written about the significant aetiological factors but there are few firm data to support the theoretical speculations.

A number of factors broadly related to personality have been suggested as predisposing individuals to anorexia nervosa. One of these, especially emphasized by Bruch (1973), is difficulty in autonomous functioning and an associated sense of ineffectiveness. Crisp (1967) has emphasized how those predisposed to develop anorexia nervosa are unprepared for maturity and how the symptoms of the disorder represent a flight from adolescent concerns and responsibilities. However, problems with autonomy and with coming to terms with adult sexuality are by no means unique to patients with anorexia nervosa; indeed, they may reflect no more than a general predisposition to psychological disorder. Both Bruch and Crisp also emphasize the compliant, perfectionist, and dependent nature of these patients' personalities. However, as Garfinkel and Garner (1982) note, it is difficult to draw meaningful conclusions about premorbid personality characteristics in a disorder with such significant and wide-ranging physical and psychological repercussions.

Eating disorders run in families. Thus the prevalence of these disorders in the relatives of patients with eating disorders has been found to be significantly higher than the expected rate in the general population (Strober & Humphrey, 1987). Gershon, Schreiber, and Hamovit (1984) found a 6 per cent lifetime morbid risk for eating disorders in the first-degree relatives of 24 patients with anorexia nervosa, compared with a 1 per cent risk in the families of normal controls. Similarly, Strober and Katz (1987) found a significant excess of eating disorders in the first- and second-degree relatives of patients with anorexia nervosa compared with non-anorexic psychiatric controls: indeed, a case of anorexia nervosa or bulimia was found in 27 per cent of the families of the patients with anorexia nervosa, compared with 6 per cent of the control families. There are also a number of reports, reviewed by Garfinkel and Garner (1982), of anorexia occurring in twins. In one rigorously conducted study of 34 pairs of twins and one set of triplets with anorexia nervosa (Holland, Hall, Murray, Russell, & Crisp, 1984), a 55 per cent concordance rate was found for identical twins compared with 7 per cent concordance for non-identical twins. In another study, a 23 per cent concordance for bulimia nervosa was found in identical twins compared to 8.7 per cent in non-identical twins (Kendler et al., 1991).

The family aggregation findings are explicable in both genetic and environmental terms. The data on the pathogenesis of family influences in the eating disorders have been reviewed by Strober and Humphrey (1987). A major problem with this work is that the findings are derived exclusively from families of patients and, as such, it is not possible to conclude anything about the causal role of any family disturbances identified. The mothers of patients with eating disorders have been described as particularly intrusive and overprotective, anxious and perfectionist, and the fathers as passive, obsessional, and ineffectual. These impressions have little empirical basis, because it has not been demonstrated that these characteristics are specific to the parents of those with eating disorders; nor, indeed, that they are present in these parents to any significant degree. Although some systematic examinations of the families of patients with bulimia have found that they perceive their families as more disturbed in various ways than do controls, it has not been shown that these perceptions are related to the eating disorder rather than to the non-specific psychological disturbance as might be found in a group of young patients with other psychological disorders. Indeed, unless some practicable means of conducting prospective research can be developed, it is unlikely that studies of the family functioning of patients with eating disorders will reveal anything significant about the aetiology of the disorder. They may well, of course, produce important findings relevant to the maintenance of these conditions and to their treatment. It has been argued that patients with eating disorders are especially likely to have had a history of sexual abuse in childhood. However, it has been found that the rate of such abuse is no greater among these patients than among patients with other psychiatric disorders.

A family history of affective disorder is common among patients with eating disorders. Thus the rate of affective disorder among the relatives of patients with anorexia nervosa is as high as among relatives of patients with depression. Preliminary evidence indicates that this association also obtains for patients with bulimia nervosa (Strober & Katz, 1987). Patients with eating disorders are also commonly found to have a personal history of affective disorder. However, a major problem with the interpretation of the findings of the latter studies is that the chronology of symptoms in patients with eating disorders is not always clear; in many cases depressive symptoms may arise as a secondary response to disturbances in eating. Nevertheless, some studies have made particularly careful analysis of the order in which symptoms have arisen. For example, Piran, Kennedy, Garfinkel, and Owens (1985) reported that among 18 patients with anorexia nervosa with a lifetime history of major depression, affective symptoms post-dated the onset of the eating disorder in 34 per cent, occurred within the same year in 22 per cent, and preceded the emergence of the eating disorder by at least one year in 44 per cent. Comparable analyses have been made with similar results in patients with bulimia (e.g. Walsh, Roose, Glassman, Gladis, & Sadik, 1985). Thus, it appears that a vulnerability to depression may increase predisposition to eating disorders, and an episode of depression may contribute to the initiation of its symptoms.

As noted above, eating disorders are especially prevalent in social subgroups where a particularly high value is placed on slim body shape. This observation, together with other related evidence, has led to considerable speculation about the role of societal pressures in the aetiology of the eating disorders (Striegel-Moore, Silbertstein, & Rodin, 1986). Indeed, the shift in societal preference towards a thinner female body shape has been offered as a possible explanation for the increasing prevalence of anorexia nervosa by leading to greater numbers of young women dieting (Garfinkel & Garner, 1982). While this explanation is highly persuasive, it is obviously not complete. Not all ballet dancers, modelling students, or young women who diet to be slim develop eating disorders, and as yet the factors that render dieters vulnerable to developing anorexia nervosa or bulimia nervosa have not been systematically investigated.

Attempts to account for the maintenance of eating disorders have proved more profitable than attempts to account for aetiology. Two views of maintenance can be distinguished. The first regards eating disorders as "closely related to" or "a form of" affective disorder. Several lines of evidence have been advanced to support this contention (Hudson, Pope, Jonas, & Yurgelun-Todd, 1983), relating to the course of these disorders, their response to certain biological tests, their phenomenology, the raised family history of affective disorder, and these patients' response to antidepressant medication. None of these lines of evidence stands up to close scrutiny (Cooper & Cooper, 1988) and there is little basis for the affective disorder view of eating disorders. There is, of course, a strong association between eating disorders and depression. However, the data suggest that a vulnerability to affective disorder may predispose individuals to develop an eating disorder, or it may contribute to its maintenance; but they do not support the idea that the eating disorders are in some sense a manifestation of an affective disorder.

The second view of maintenance derives from a cognitive behavioural conceptualization of the eating disorders. The argument for such a view of anorexia nervosa and bulimia nervosa has been extensively elaborated in earlier reviews (Fairburn, Cooper, & Cooper 1986; Garner & Bemis, 1982). The essential tenet of this view is that the central psychopathological disturbance in these patients is the overvalued ideas about weight and shape. Indeed, it is argued, most of the other clinical features of these disorders can be understood in terms of this core psychopathology. According to this view, the belief that shape and weight are of fundamental importance and must be kept under strict control is not merely symptomatic of these disorders but is of primary importance in their maintenance. The specific features of eating disorders, such as frequent weighing, sensitivity to changes in shape and weight, extreme dieting, self-induced vomiting and purgative abuse, and abnormal attitudes towards food and eating, are also presented as comprehensible given these core beliefs concerning shape and weight.

The cognitive behavioural account of eating disorders regards the relatively uniform beliefs and values of these patients as implicit unarticulated rules by which they assign meaning and value to their experience. The way they evaluate themselves and their behaviour, their perceptions, and aspirations, are regarded as being determined by these values. Thus their self-worth is seen as being evaluated largely in terms of their shape and weight: they view fatness as odious and reprehensible, they see slimness as attractive and desirable, and the maintenance of self-control is of prime importance. In addition, some attach extreme importance to weight loss. It is clear that such beliefs are not radically different from views that are widely held and reinforced by prevailing social values. They differ from these more generally held attitudes by being exaggerated, rigidly held and imbued with great personal significance; it is these qualities, it is argued, which make them dysfunctional. It is further argued that the absolute and exaggerated nature of these concerns about shape and weight reflects the operation of certain dysfunctional styles of reasoning, similar to those described as operating in depression. The cognitive behavioural conceptualization of eating disorders has considerable prima facie validity, but there is little direct evidence to support it.

Bulimic episodes present two problems for a cognitive behavioural view of eating disorders. First, given these patients' implicit values concerning shape and weight, it would be predicted that their fear of weight gain would simply lead to constant dieting, with success reinforcing further dietary restriction. Second, it would be predicted that, if for some reason a patient did break the diet, the patient would simply recommence dieting. The clinical features of bulimia nervosa and of the bulimic subgroup of patients with anorexia nervosa are not consistent with either of these predictions. These patients do not successfully adhere to their dietary regimes, and when their diets are broken, rather than minimizing the indiscretion, they go to the other extreme and overeat. It has been argued that it is dietary restriction itself that is responsible for the episodes of loss of control over eating, and that the link between dieting and bulimic episodes is a cognitive one (Polivy & Herman, 1985). It has been found in laboratory research that, under certain predictable circumstances, subjects who are restricting their food intake will overeat or "counter-regulate". One such circumstance is the belief that certain dietary rules have been transgressed: that is, in contrast to unrestrained eaters, restrained eaters tend to eat more following the prior consumption of a large number of calories than following a small number of calories. This effect has also been produced by simply manipulating the subjects' beliefs about the calorie content of the previously consumed food. Other factors found to produce counter-regulation in dieters are dysphoric mood states and the consumption of alcohol. Once the cognitive constraints on eating are removed by some disinhibiting factor, hunger and other physiological forces aimed at correcting the deprivation take over and lead to overeating. This essentially laboratory phenomenon has been presented as an analogy for bulimic episodes. Despite the intuitive appeal of this analogy, there is no clear and direct evidence to support the causal role of dietary restraint in the aetiology of bulimic episodes, and it remains wholly unclear what the conditions are that render individuals vulnerable to dietary disinhibition and bulimic episodes (Cooper & Charnock, 1990).

TREATMENT

Although much has been written about the treatment of anorexia nervosa, there has been little controlled research into the management of this disorder. Such research that has been done has produced largely negative findings. Thus, both the appetite-stimulating antihistamine drug cyproheptadine and the tricyclic antidepressant amitryptyline have been shown to add nothing in terms of weight gain to routine nursing care (Halmi, Eckert, LaDu, & Cohen, 1986), and the antidepressant clomipramine has been shown to be equally unhelpful (Lacey & Crisp, 1980). Similarly negative conclusions have emerged from studies of psychological methods of intervention. Thus, a behaviour modification regime has been found to confer no benefit to short-term weight gain when compared to milieu therapy (Eckert, Goldberg, Halmi, Casper, & Davis, 1979); and, similarly, a strict operant regime has been shown to be no better at promoting weight gain than a more lenient regime (Touyz, Beumont, & Glaun, 1984). The single exception to these negative conclusions derives from an investigation of family therapy (Russell, Szmuckler, Dare, & Eisler, 1987). In a study in which, following a period of inpatient weight restoration, patients received one year of either family therapy or individual therapy, the family therapy was found to be superior, especially for non-chronic patients with an early age of onset.

The mainstay of treatment for anorexia nervosa has been hospitalization and nursing care (Crisp, 1965; Garfinkel & Garner, 1982; Russell, 1970). Essentially these treatments involve the re-feeding of patients coupled with nutritional education. All the authorities cited catalogue a number of strategies for dealing with particular aspects of these patients' care, such as their tendency to induce vomiting, hide food, engage in secret exercising, and so on. The short-term results of such an approach are good and most patients can be restored to a healthy body weight within three or four months. However, improvement in other aspects of the disorder is less impressive. In the Maudsley study cited above (Russell et al., 1987), after inpatient weight restoration and a year of therapy (family or individual) only 23 per cent were classified as having a good outcome and 60 per cent as having a poor outcome. The Maudsley is a tertiary referral centre and these disappointing figures are not typical. Thus, a two-year follow-up of patients treated in the

Toronto General Hospital revealed that 50 per cent of the patients had a good outcome and only 16 per cent a poor outcome (Kennedy, Kaplan, & Garfinkel, 1992).

An innovation in the management of anorexia nervosa has been the description of a day-patient treatment programme (Piran & Kaplan, 1990). There are both clinical and financial advantages to such an outpatient setting. A detailed programme has been specified and preliminary accounts of its efficacy are encouraging: close to 70 per cent of patients demonstrate at least a moderate outcome and clinical gains appear to be well maintained six months following discharge.

Despite the fact that bulimia nervosa was not identified as a distinct disorder until the end of the 1970s, there have been a remarkable number of systematic evaluations of specific forms of treatment (Fairburn et al., 1991). Two lines of work have gone on largely independently. The first has concerned the efficacy of medication. A number of double-blind controlled trials have been conducted of the efficacy of a variety of antidepressant drugs. The studies have involved mainly standard tricyclic medication such as imipramine and desipramine. These studies have all been rather restricted in scope in that only a limited range of the psychopathology has been assessed, and rarely has attention been paid to the maintenance of change and the effects of discontinuation of drug treatment. There are four principal conclusions that can be drawn from the studies (Fairburn et al., 1992). First, antidepressant drugs are superior to placebo (inactive dummy pills) at reducing the frequency of bulimic episodes and improving related clinical features; they also have a beneficial effect on the general psychopathology. Second, the clinical impact of drugs is modest: although most patients reduce the frequency of bulimic episodes, at the end of a course of treatment most are still experiencing bulimic episodes and few could be regarded as eating normally. Third, no consistent predictors of response have been identified and, in particular, the level of depressive symptomatology does not predict outcome. Finally, the two studies that have examined maintenance of change on medication and response to discontinuation (Pyle et al., 1990; Walsh, Hadigan, Devlin, Gladis, & Roose, 1991) have revealed that relapse is common, even with patients continuing to take the medication. There has been interest in the efficacy of the new generation of antidepressants, the selective serotonin re-uptake inhibitors. It is clear that this class of drugs has a significant positive clinical effect in these patients. However, this effect appears to be no greater than that obtained using far less expensive tricyclic medication; and there is no evidence suggesting that it is especially appropriate for patients with a particular clinical profile.

The second line of research has concerned the efficacy of certain psychological treatments. Most of the studies have involved an assessment of a cognitive behavioural approach to the management of bulimia nervosa. This form of treatment, which has been comprehensively described (Fairburn &

Cooper, 1989), is generally delivered on an individual basis to outpatients over the course of four to five months. A consistent finding of the treatment studies is that this treatment produces marked reductions in the frequency of episodes of bulimia and purging. In addition, there is an improvement in the other aspects of the specific psychopathology, such as attitudes to shape and weight and dietary restraint, as well as improvements in general mental state and social functioning. Maintenance of change, at least up to one year, is good (Fairburn, Kirk, O'Connor, & Cooper, 1986; Fairburn et al., 1991). Longer-term maintenance has not yet been reported. Cognitive behaviour therapy for bulimia nervosa has been compared with other forms of brief psychological management. Comparisons with a purely behavioural approach have consistently favoured the cognitive behavioural condition. However, in two studies other focal psychotherapies emerged as just as effective (Fairburn, Kirk, O'Connor, & Cooper, 1986; Fairburn et al., 1991), notably a form of interpersonal psychotherapy.

There have been only two reports in which cognitive behaviour therapy has been compared with antidepressant medication in the treatment of bulimia nervosa (Agras et al., 1992; Mitchell et al., 1990). In both, psychological treatment alone was markedly superior to the drug alone. Both studies included a combined treatment condition. In the Minneapolis study (Mitchell et al., 1990), the outcome of patients receiving both the psychological treatment and imipramine was the same as for those who only received the psychological treatment; but in the Stanford study (Agras et al., 1992), there was some benefit from combining the two treatments. It is unclear what accounts for this difference and further studies of combination treatment are required. An important clinical question, particularly since cognitive behaviour therapy is an expensive specialist treatment, is whether an antidepressant could enhance a cheaper simpler treatment. Indeed, it has been suggested that cognitive behaviour therapy may well constitute overtreatment for many patients and, in view of this, a stepped care approach has been recommended. This has yet to be evaluated.

COURSE AND OUTCOME

A number of studies have been conducted of the course and outcome of anorexia nervosa. The overall findings indicate that about one-third of patients recover completely, one-third have a moderate outcome, and one-third remain severely ill (Hsu, 1990). The results have been published of a 20-year follow-up study of 41 patients treated for anorexia nervosa at the Maudsley hospital between 1959 and 1966 (Ratnasuria, Eisler, Szmukler, & Russell, 1991). This study highlights the very serious nature of the disorder when it takes a chronic course. After 20 years, almost 40 per cent of the patients were still gravely incapacitated by the illness or had died. Indeed, an alarming and consistent finding of the outcome studies is that the mortality rate for anorexia nervosa is around 15 per cent (Hsu, 1990). In the Maudsley sample all the deaths (i.e., 14.6 per cent), with one exception, were attributable to anorexia nervosa. Of these, half were due to suicide and the remainder to complications of the illness associated with electrolyte imbalance. Factors associated with a poor prognosis were a later age of onset of the disorder, a history of neurotic and personality disturbances, disturbed relationships in the family and a longer duration of illness. The outcome of mild cases of the disorder is unknown but likely to be considerably more favourable.

Little is known about the course and outcome of bulimia nervosa. There have been no systematic studies of the natural history of the disorder. The reports of outcome following treatment have been limited in that the full range of psychopathological disturbance has rarely been reported and follow-up has been short term. As noted, two studies have revealed that relapse is the likely outcome when tricyclic medication is withdrawn and, indeed, even when patients are maintained on medication (Pyle et al., 1990; Walsh et al., 1991). There have been more encouraging reports of the short-term outcome following a relatively brief course of psychological treatment (e.g. Fairburn, Kirk, O'Connor, & Cooper, 1986; Fairburn et al., 1993). In a review of the outcome studies, Hsu (1990) has noted that, while outcome varies consider-ably across samples, overall at least two-thirds of patients receiving treatment no longer fulfil the diagnostic criteria at one-year follow-up. The population of patients with bulimia nervosa appears to be heterogeneous with respect to prognosis, and longitudinal clinical and epidemiological research is required to determine the profile of outcomes of these patients and to identify prognostic indicators.

FURTHER READING

Garfinkel, P. E., & Garner, D. M. (1982). *Anorexia nervosa: A multidimensional perspective*. New York: Basic Books.
Garner, D. M., & Garfinkel, P. E. (1985). *Handbook of psychotherapy for anorexia nervosa and bulimia nervosa*. New York: Guilford.
Hsu, L. K. (1990). *Eating disorders*. New York: Guilford.
Russell, G. F. M. (1979). Bulimia nervosa: An ominous variant of anorexia nervosa. *Psychological Medicine, 9*, 429–448.

REFERENCES

Agras, W. S., Rossiter, E. M., Arnow, B., Schneider, J. A., Telch, C. F., Raeburn, S. D., Bruce, B., Perl, M., & Koran, L. M. (1992). Pharmacologic and cognitive-behavioral treatment for bulimia nervosa: A controlled trial. *American Journal of Psychiatry, 149*, 82–87.
American Psychiatric Association (1980). *Diagnostic and statistical manual of mental disorders* (3rd edn). Washington, DC: APA.

American Psychiatric Association (1987). *Diagnostic and statistical manual of mental disorders* (3rd edn, revised). Washington, DC: APA.

American Psychiatric Association (1991). *DSM-IV Options Book: Diagnostic and statistical manual of mental disorders.* Washington, DC: APA.

Bruch, H. (1973). *Eating disorders. Obesity, anorexia nervosa, and the person within.* New York: Basic Books.

Carlat, D. J., & Camargo, C. A. (1991). Review of bulimia nervosa in males. *American Journal of Psychiatry, 148,* 831–843.

Cooper, P. J. (1993). *Bulimia nervosa: A guide to recovery.* London: Robinson.

Cooper, P. J., & Charnock, D. (1990). From restraint to bulimic episodes: A problem of some loose connections. *Appetite, 14,* 120–122.

Cooper, P. J., & Cooper, Z. (1988). Eating disorders. In E. Miller & P. J. Cooper (Eds) *Adult abnormal psychology* (pp. 268–298). Edinburgh: Churchill Livingstone.

Cooper, P. J., & Fairburn, C. G. (1986). The depressive symptoms of bulimia nervosa. *British Journal of Psychiatry, 148,* 268–274.

Cooper, P. J., & Taylor, M. J. (1988). Body image disturbance in bulimia nervosa. *British Journal of Psychiatry, 153,* 32–36.

Cooper, P. J., Charnock, D. J., & Taylor, M. J. (1987). The prevalence of bulimia nervosa: A replication study. *British Journal of Psychiatry, 151,* 684–686.

Crisp, A. H. (1965). A treatment regime for anorexia nervosa. *British Journal of Psychiatry, 30,* 279–286.

Crisp, A. H. (1967). Anorexia nervosa. *Hospital Medicine, 1,* 713–718.

Crisp, A. H., Palmer, R. L., & Kalucy, R. S. (1976). How common is anorexia nervosa? A prevalence study. *British Journal of Psychiatry, 128,* 548–549.

Eckert, E. D., Goldberg, S. C., Halmi, K. A., Casper, R. C., & Davis, J. M. (1979). Behaviour therapy in anorexia nervosa. *British Journal of Psychiatry, 134,* 55–59.

Fairburn, C. G., & Beglin, S. (1991). Studies of the epidemiology of bulimia nervosa. *American Journal of Psychiatry, 147,* 401–408.

Fairburn, C. G., & Cooper, P. J. (1984). The clinical features of bulimia nervosa. *British Journal of Psychiatry, 144,* 238–246.

Fairburn, C. G., & Cooper, P. J. (1989). The cognitive-behavioural treatment of eating disorders. In K. Hawton, P. Salkovskis, J. Kirk, & D. M. Clark (Eds) *Cognitive-behavioural approaches to adult psychiatric disorders. A practical guide* (pp. 277–314). Oxford: Oxford University Press.

Fairburn, C. G., Agras, W. S., & Wilson, G. T. (1992). The research on the treatment of bulimia nervosa: Practical and theoretical implications. In G. H. Anderson & S. H. Kennedy (Eds) *The biology of feast and famine. Relevance to eating disorders* (pp. 317–340). New York: Academic Press.

Fairburn, C. G., Cooper, Z., & Cooper, P. J. (1986). The clinical features and maintenance of bulimia nervosa. In K. D. Brownell & J. P. Foreyt (Eds) *Handbook of eating disorders. Physiology, psychology and treatment of eating disorders* (pp. 389–404). New York: Basic Books.

Fairburn, C. G., Kirk, J., O'Connor, M., & Cooper, P. J. (1986). A comparison of two psychological treatments for bulimia nervosa. *Behaviour Research and Therapy, 24,* 629–643.

Fairburn, C. G., Jones, R., Peveler, R. C., Carr, S. J., Solomon, R. A., O'Connor, M. E., Burton, J., & Hope, R. A. (1991). Three psychological treatments for bulimia nervosa: A comparative trial. *Archives of General Psychiatry, 48,* 463–469.

Garfinkel, P. E., & Garner, D. M. (1982). *Anorexia nervosa. A multidimensional perspective.* New York: Basic Books.

Garfinkel, P. E., Modlofsky, H., & Garner, D. M. (1980). The heterogeneity of anorexia nervosa. *Archives of General Psychiatry, 37*, 1036–1040.

Garner, D. M., & Bemis, K. M. (1982). A cognitive behavior approach to anorexia nervosa. *Cognitive Therapy and Research, 6*, 1–27.

Garner, D. M., Rockert, W., Olmsted, M. P., Johnson, C., & Coscina, D. V. (1985). Psychoeducational principles in the treatment of bulimia and anorexia nervosa. In D. M. Garner & P. E. Garfinkel (Eds) *Handbook of psychotherapy for anorexia nervosa and bulimia nervosa* (pp. 513–572). New York: Guilford.

Gershon, E. S., Schreiber, J. L., & Hamovit, J. R. (1984). Clinical findings in patients with anorexia nervosa and affective illness and their relatives. *American Journal of Psychiatry, 141*, 1419–1422.

Halmi, K. A., Eckert, E., LaDu, T. J., & Cohen J. (1986). Anorexia nervosa; Treatment efficacy of cyproheptadine and amitriptyline. *Archives of General Psychiatry, 43*, 177–181.

Holland, A. J., Hall, A., Murray, R., Russell, G. F. M., & Crisp, A. H. (1984). Anorexia nervosa: A study of 34 twin pairs and one set of triplets. *British Journal of Psychiatry, 145*, 414–418.

Hsu, L. K. (1990). *Eating disorders*. New York: Guilford.

Hudson, J. I., Pope, H. G., Jonas, J. M., & Yurgelun-Todd, D. (1983). Family history study of anorexia nervosa and bulimia. *British Journal of Psychiatry, 142*, 133–138.

Kendell, R. E., Hall, D. J., Hailey, A., & Babigian, H. M. (1973). The epidemiology of anorexia nervosa. *Psychological Medicine, 3*, 200–203.

Kendler, K. S., McLean, C., Neale, M., Kessler, R., Heath, A., & Eaves, L. (1991). The genetic epidemiology of bulimia nervosa. *American Journal of Psychiatry, 148*, 1627–1637.

Kennedy, S., Kaplan, A., & Garfinkel, P. (1992). Intensive hospital treatment for anorexia nervosa and bulimia. In P. J. Cooper & A. Stein (Eds) *Monographs in clinical paediatrics. Feeding problems and eating disorders in children and adolescents* (pp. 161–181). New York: Harwood.

Lacey, J. H., & Crisp, A. H. (1980). Hunger, food intake and weight: The impact of clomipramine on a refeeding anorexia nervosa population. *Postgraduate Medical Journal, 56*, 79–85.

Lask, B., & Bryant-Waugh, R. (1992). Childhood onset anorexia nervosa and related eating disorders. *Journal of Child Psychology and Psychiatry, 3*, 281–300.

Lucas, A. R., Beard, C. M., O'Fallon, W. M., & Kurland, L. T. (1991). 50-year trends in the incidence of anorexia nervosa in Rochester, Minneapolis: A population based study. *American Journal of Psychiatry, 148*, 917–922.

Mann, A. H., Wakeling, A., Wood, U., Monck, E., Dobbs, R., & Szmukler, G. I. (1983). Screening for abnormal eating attitudes of psychiatric morbidity in an unselected population of 15 year old school girls. *Psychological Medicine, 13*, 573–580.

Mitchell, J. E. (1986a). Anorexia nervosa: Medical and physiological aspects. In K. D. Brownell & J. P. Foreyt (Eds) *Handbook of eating disorders. Physiology, psychology and treatment of obesity, anorexia and bulimia* (pp. 247–265). New York: Basic Books.

Mitchell, J. E. (1986b). Bulimia: Medical and physiological aspects. In K. D. Brownell & J. P. Foreyt (Eds) *Handbook of eating disorders: Physiology, psychology and treatment of obesity, anorexia and bulimia* (pp. 379–388). New York: Basic Books.

Mitchell, J. E., Pyle, R. L., Eckert, E. D., Hatsukami, D., Pomeroy, C., & Zimmerman, R. (1990). A comparison study of antidepressants and structured intensive group psychotherapy in the treatment of bulimia nervosa. *Archives of General Psychiatry*, *47*, 149–157.

Piran, N., & Kaplan, A. S. (1990). *A day hospital group treatment program for anorexia nervosa and bulimia nervosa*. New York: Brunner/Mazel.

Piran, N., Kennedy, S., Garfinkel, P. E., & Owens, M. (1985). Affective disturbance in eating disorders. *Journal of Nervous and Mental Disease*, *173*, 395–400.

Polivy, J., & Herman, C. P. (1985). Dieting and tingeing: Causal analysis. *American Psychologist*, *40*, 193–201.

Pyle, R. L., Mitchell, J. E., Eckert, E. D., Hatsukami, D., Pomeroy, C., & Zimmerman, R. (1990). Maintenance treatment and six month outcome for bulimia patients who respond to initial treatment. *American Journal of Psychiatry*, *147*, 871–875.

Rastam, M., Gillberg, C., & Garton, M. (1989). Anorexia nervosa in a Swedish urban region: A population based study. *British Journal of Psychiatry*, *155*, 642–646.

Ratnasuria, R. H., Eisler, I., Szmukler, G., & Russell, G. F. M. (1991). Anorexia nervosa: Outcome and prognostic factors after 20 years. *British Journal of Psychiatry*, *158*, 495–502.

Russell, G. F. M. (1970). Anorexia nervosa: Its identity as an illness and its treatment. In J. H Price (Ed.) *Modern trends in psychological medicine* (pp. 131–164). London: Butterworths.

Russell, G. F. M. (1979). Bulimia nervosa: An ominous variant of anorexia nervosa. *Psychological Medicine*, *9*, 429–448.

Russell, G. F. M., Szmuckler, G. I., Dare, C., & Eisler, I. (1987). An evaluation of family therapy in anorexia nervosa and bulimia nervosa. *Archives of General Psychiatry*, *44*, 1047–1056.

Schotte, D. E., & Stunkard, A. J. (1987). Bulimia vs bulimic behaviors on a college campus. *Journal of the American Medical Association*, *258*, 1213–1215.

Steere, J. A., Butler, G., & Cooper, P. J. (1990). The anxiety symptoms of bulimia nervosa: A comparative study. *International Journal of Eating Disorders*, *9*, 293–301.

Striegel-Moore, R. H., Silbertstein, L. R., & Rodin, J. (1986). Toward an understanding of risk factors for bulimia. *American Psychologist*, *41*, 246–265.

Strober, M., & Humphrey, L. (1987). Familial contributions to the etiology and course of anorexia nervosa and bulimia. *Journal of Consulting and Clinical Psychology*, *55*, 656–659.

Strober, M., & Katz, J. L. (1987). Do eating disorders and affective disorders share a common etiology? *International Journal of Eating Disorders*, *6*, 171–180.

Szmukler, G. I., McCance, C., McCrone, L., & Hunter, D. (1986). A psychiatric case register study from Aberdeen. *Psychological Medicine*, *16*, 49–58.

Touyz, S. W., Beumont, P. J. V., & Glaun, D. (1984). A comparison of lenient and strict operant conditioning programmes in refeeding patients with anorexia nervosa. *British Journal of Psychiatry*, *144*, 517–520.

Walsh, B. T., Hadigan, C. M., Devlin, M. J., Gladis, M., & Roose, S. P. (1991). Long-term outcome of anti-depressant treatment for bulimia nervosa. *American Journal of Psychiatry*, *148*, 1206–1212.

Walsh, B. T., Kissileff, H. R., Cassidy, S. M., & Danzic, S. (1989). Eating behavior of women with bulimia. *Archives of General Psychiatry*, *46*, 54–58.

Walsh, B. T., Roose, S. P., Glassman, A. H., Gladis, M. A., & Sadik, C. (1985). Depression and bulimia. *Psychosomatic Medicine*, *47*, 123–131.

ALCOHOL AND DRUG ADDICTION

Geoffrey Lowe
University of Hull, England

Psychology and its allied behavioural disciplines have been increasingly recognized for their contributions in helping to understand addiction and its treatment. In these research programmes we have seen an emerging integration of biological, psychological, and sociological approaches to aetiology and treatment. In this chapter I shall highlight this biopsychosocial model, together with perspectives based on social-learning theory and on cognitive principles.

Does addiction to various drugs involve different processes, each specific to a particular drug type (that is, individual theories)? Or is there some general process that different drug addictions have in common (that is, a unitary theory)? Many theories embrace a commonalities approach for a variety of addictive behaviours, but emphasize alcohol abuse and alcoholism – the most costly of addiction problems in terms of frequency of abuse and potential for harm.

I shall proceed by first looking at alcohol as a major psychoactive drug. Many of the basic observations about alcohol-behaviour interactions have implications for dependence (or alcoholism). Next I shall consider various approaches to the specific aetiology of alcoholism and its treatment, before looking at drug dependence in general as an addictive process.

ALCOHOL

Alcohol is the major social drug, with interesting psychoactive properties. One of its first effects is on the central nervous system, the higher centres related to judgement, inhibition, and the like. What is more important is what this feels like, how it is experienced. With mild intoxication comes relaxation, a more carefree feeling. It is generally experienced as a plus, a high; pre-existing tensions are relieved. A good mood can be accentuated: alcohol is experienced as a mood changer in a positive direction. This capacity of alcohol is one factor to remember in trying to understand use sufficient for addiction.

In the field of psychopharmacology, researchers have found the effects of alcohol a useful tool in the study of fundamental psychological mechanisms, while others have been interested in such research for clinical reasons. Consequently, the psychopharmacology of alcohol as a research area has expanded rapidly in breadth and depth. Certainly the experimental investigation of alcohol's effects on the central nervous system and behaviour, and of the alcohol dependence process, has achieved a good measure of scientific respectability.

ALCOHOL INTOXICATION

Alcohol is a depressant agent, capable of impairing, retarding, and disorganizing the functions of the central nervous system (CNS). Nevertheless, many of the overt behavioural effects of alcohol are stimulant. The behaviourally arousing effects of alcohol arise partly because CNS inhibitory processes tend to be more susceptible to disruption than the excitatory processes. A further contribution to the behavioural stimulation caused by alcohol is a compensatory response, counteracting the depressant drug effect.

Subjective reports of intoxication are important because they provide

Table 1 Typical effects at different levels of blood-alcohol concentration (BAC)

BAC (mg/100 ml)	Psychological/clinical effects*
20	Negligible
30	Possible slight flushing and a little more talkative than usual
50	Relaxation, lowering of inhibitions; impaired attention, impaired vigilance
60–99	Impaired sensory function; motor incoordination; changes in mood and behaviour (mild euphoria, self-satisfaction, louder profuse speech); impaired mental activity
100	Significant feelings of intoxication; impaired short-term memory
150	Staggering; lengthened reaction time; marked impairment on mental and psycho-motor tests; slurred speech
200	Insensitivity to stimuli; extreme clumsiness; nausea and vomiting
250	Marked tendency to pass out
300	Hypothermia; amnesia; anaesthesia; slow, heavy breathing
400	Comatose
500	Breathing abolished; death

Note: *These approximations are given for determinations obtained during *rising* BACs. During this period the mental effects are more pronounced and the mood tends to be more euphoric. On the other hand, as BAC declines, at equivalent levels the mental effects are less pronounced, and more negative feeling tones are experienced

access to the subjective cues that govern drinking behaviour in a single drinking session. However, the meaning or intensity of subjective intoxication varies greatly according to dose level and drinking habits. Although subjective ratings (SR) and BAC (blood-alcohol concentration) correspond quite closely while BAC is rising, as BAC decreases the disparity between BAC and SR becomes marked, with SR declining much faster. This means that people may *feel* quite sober, even when they still have significant BACs.

EFFECTS ON HUMAN PERFORMANCE

There is little doubt that alcohol can affect various aspects of human performance. But when we ask more precise questions about which kinds of tasks, under what conditions, and under what dosages, then a whole variety of factors come into play. These include differences in subject population (for example, sex, weight, age, and type of drinker); differences in methods of alcohol administration; different types of alcohol; temporal variations (for example, consumption period, time of day, time between ingestion and testing); and different tasks and demand characteristics.

In general, cognitive and perceptual-sensory performances are most disrupted by alcohol; psycho-motor tasks seem to be more resistant, although measurable decrements are usually observed. Moskowitz (1979) and others have reported the sensitivity of attention, perception, and information processing to moderate and even low doses of alcohol and related drugs. Since these are the areas of crucial importance for skills performance in complex human–machine interactions, such findings explain why activities such as driving are so susceptible to alcohol-induced disruption.

Alcohol intoxication also interferes with memory and learning processes. The most severe memory disturbance is the alcoholic "blackout", an inability to recall events that happened during a drinking episode, even though consciousness was neither significantly clouded nor lost. We may observe poorer recall at BACs of 40 mg/dl, and it seems to worsen in a linear fashion as BAC rises.

One of the major difficulties in determining and explaining these memory deficits is that the effects of acute intoxication wear off after a few hours, leaving the person in a different physiological state. What is learned while intoxicated is not so well recalled when tested under a sober state (and vice versa). Retention is, however, greater when the original drug state is reinstated (Lowe, 1981, 1988). *State-dependent learning* (SDL) is the term used to describe this phenomenon. Such "dissociation" of learning between drunk and sober states has led to the speculation that SDL may be a factor in the aetiology of alcoholism (see below).

ALCOHOLISM

There is no single definition of alcoholism, but several behavioural criteria taken together enable one to judge the severity of a drinking problem. Among these criteria are "loss-of-control" (of drinking behaviour); psychological dependence ("needs a drink" to get anything done); loss of job(s), family, or friends because of drinking; blackouts; increasing tolerance for alcohol; withdrawal symptoms upon stopping drinking (physical dependence).

Most psychologists prefer the terms *alcohol dependence* or *problem drinking* to refer to the excessive and compulsive use of alcohol, since the label "alcoholism" is too closely associated with a simple disease model (see below). But for convenience I shall use these terms interchangeably to refer to a condition determined by a host of influences rather than a static all-or-none entity.

We need to understand how chronic and excessive alcohol drinking is generated, as well as the conditions under which such over-indulgence can be attenuated and prevented.

Why do people drink?

Any useful theoretical model for drinking behaviour must address at least three questions. First, why do people start drinking? Second, what factors maintain drinking? Third, why do some drink so much as to develop serious problems?

Psychological approaches

Psychological formulations of dependence, like the definitions of the World Health Organization (WHO) and the American Psychiatric Association's DSM-III (*Diagnostic and Statistical Manual of Mental Disorders*), generally imply that dependence is a mental or behavioural disorder whose origins are as much environmental as they are physical (Babor & Lauerman, 1986). Three definitions that convey some of the variety of psychological approaches to dependence are those proposed by psychoanalysts, behaviourists, and family interaction theorists.

In the *psychoanalytic model*, dependence is seen as a symptom of some underlying psychological conflict or pre-alcoholic personality type. *Behavioural* definitions, on the other hand, emphasize the environmental conditions that initiate and maintain drinking behaviour, avoiding assumptions about physical or psychological causes of a disease process. *Family interaction* theorists define dependence as a family illness, and give primary emphasis to the alcohol or drug user's interpersonal relationships.

The tension-reduction hypothesis

Historically one of the first models proposed to explain drinking was termed the tension-reduction hypothesis, or TRH (Conger, 1956), which holds that people drink alcohol primarily because of its tension-reducing effects. This hypothesis has much intuitive appeal, because alcohol is a sedative drug that leads to relaxation and slowed reactions.

However, alcohol's effects on physiological processes are not simple, which creates difficulties for a simple version of the TRH. Moreover, in a longitudinal study of a heavy social drinker, Rohsenow (1982) found that drinking occurred for reasons of attaining a positive state of affect rather than avoiding a negative state of tension.

Two reformulations of the TRH seem to be more viable. Sher and Levenson (1982) discovered that high levels of alcohol consumption decrease the strength of responses to stress. This decrease was termed the *stress-response-dampening* (SRD) effect. It was found that people who had been drinking did not respond as strongly as non-drinking subjects to either physiological or psychological stresses. So that, rather than tension reduction, alcohol may produce tension avoidance, and that high-risk drinkers are more likely to experience this effect than others.

A second reformulation, proposed by Hull (1981), is based on social psychological theories of self-awareness. He suggests that alcohol can interfere with cognition to make thought more superficial and decrease negative self-feedback that would otherwise produce tension.

The disease model

The most influential model during much of the twentieth century has been the disease conception of alcoholism. Among psychiatric and other medically oriented treatment programmes, this model still predominates, although since the early 1980s the disease model has become much less influential among psychologically based treatment programmes.

Throughout history, isolated attempts have been made to describe alcohol intoxication as a disease, but not until the late 1930s and early 1940s did this view become popular. The disease model of alcoholism was elevated to scientific respectability by the pioneering work of E. M. Jellinek, who defined alcoholism as "any use of alcoholic beverages that causes any damage to the individual or society or both" (1960). Damage was conceived broadly as physiological, psychological, social, or even financial. This sweeping conception of alcoholism enabled Jellinek to identify several different "species" or types of alcoholism.

The distinguishing mark of gamma alcoholism is loss of control. In addition, gamma alcoholism is characterised by increased tissue tolerance, adaptive cell metabolism, and withdrawal symptoms. These four elements add up to physical dependency and, ultimately, serious organic damage.

Delta alcoholism also features the latter three elements but there is no loss of control and the pattern of drinking is different. Rather than losing control, the delta alcoholic has an inability to abstain.

The alcohol dependence syndrome

A later conception of the disease model is the alcohol dependence syndrome (Edwards, 1986). This model grew out of some dissatisfaction with the term "alcoholism" and with the traditional concept of alcoholism as a disease. The word "syndrome" adds flexibility to the disease model because it suggests a group of concurrent behaviours that accompany alcohol dependence. The behaviours need not always be observed in an individual, nor do they need to be observable to the same degree in everyone who is alcohol dependent. Thus the concepts of loss of control and inability to abstain, with their all-or-none connotation, do not apply to the alcohol dependence syndrome. Instead, the term "impaired control" is used to suggest that people drink heavily because, at certain times and for a variety of psychological and physiological reasons, they choose not to exercise control.

There are seven essential elements in the alcohol dependence syndrome. First is a narrowing of drinking repertoire. The dependent person gradually begins to drink the same, whether it is a workday, a weekend, or a holiday, whether in a depressed or happy mood. Second is a salience of drink-seeking behaviour, meaning that drinking begins to take top priority over all other aspects of life. A third element is increased tolerance. Alcohol does not produce as much tolerance as some other drugs, but the dependent person often becomes accustomed to going about his or her business at drug levels that would incapacitate the non-tolerant drinker.

A fourth element of the alcohol dependence syndrome is withdrawal symptoms – depending on length and amount of use. Fifth is the relief or avoidance of withdrawal symptoms by further drinking. Sixth is the subjective awareness of the compulsion to drink. Dependent drinkers may fight against the compulsion, but they drink anyway. A final element of the alcohol dependence syndrome is reinstatement of dependence after abstinence. When drinking cues are removed, as in a treatment centre, patients often find abstinence surprisingly easy. However, if abstinence is broken, dependency is reinstated. Time of reinstatement is inversely related to degree of dependence, meaning that moderately dependent drinkers may take months, while severely dependent patients may resume full dependency in as little as three days.

Simple disease models have now been largely replaced by a more complex set of working hypotheses based, not on irreversible physiological processes, but on learning and conditioning, motivation and self-regulation, expectations and attributions.

The social learning model

Many psychologists have accepted social learning theory as offering the most useful explanation for why people begin to drink, continue in moderation, or drink in a harmful manner. Social learning theory conceives of problem drinking as a multiply determined, learned behaviour disorder. It can be understood best through the empirically derived principles of social learning, cognitive psychology, and behaviour therapies.

People begin to drink, according to social learning theory, for at least three reasons. First, the taste of alcohol and/or its immediate effect may be pleasurable (positive reinforcement); second, a person may decide earlier that drinking alcohol is consistent with personal standards (cognitive mediation); and third, one may learn to drink through observing others (modelling). Any one or combination of these factors is sufficient to initiate and control drinking behaviour.

The social learning model also offers several explanations for why people drink too much. Excessive drinking may serve as a coping response. In other words, although alcohol acts as a depressant, the initial effect of small doses is often interpreted by drinkers as a means of strengthening their ability to cope. This response to alcohol gives drinkers a sense of power and also a feeling of avoiding responsibility or minimizing stress. People will then continue to drink as long as they perceive the desirable effects of alcohol.

Modelling also provides an explanation for heavy drinking. Heavy-drinking models do produce increased consumption – especially in drinkers with a prior history of heavy drinking.

A third explanation for excessive drinking offered by the social learning model is based on the principles of *negative reinforcement*. Most heavy drinkers have learned that they can avoid or reduce the painful effects of withdrawal symptoms by maintaining blood-alcohol concentrations at a particular level. As this level begins to drop, the alcohol addict feels the discomfort of withdrawal. These symptoms can be avoided by ingesting more alcohol; thus negative reinforcement increases the likelihood that heavy drinking will be continued.

The cognitive social learning approach

The cognitive social learning approach (Marlatt & Donovan, 1982) additionally emphasizes cognitive processes and expectations (see also Hodgson, 1990). The individual's expectancies about alcohol and its anticipated effects can influence drinking and a number of related behaviours (Brown, Goldman, & Christiansen, 1985). Such cognitive expectancies appear to override the pharmacologic effects of alcohol for a variety of human behaviours in which one's beliefs about alcohol are influential (Critchlow, 1986; Goldman, Brown, & Christiansen, 1987; Lowe, 1990).

The behavioural perspectives of these social learning theories not only provide explanations for why people drink, but also suggest a variety of treatment techniques to help people overcome excessive drinking habits. Since drinking behaviour is learned, it can be unlearned or relearned. People can learn to abstain from alcohol completely, or they can learn to moderate their intake. The social learning model therefore is not tied to the goal of abstinence, but can accommodate either controlled drinking or abstinence as a treatment goal. Useful interventions could be directed towards the development of social skills, both generalized and specific, to high-risk drinking situations, perceived control and enhanced personal efficacy, and relapse-prevention techniques.

Is alcoholism hereditary?

The notion that alcoholism is hereditary dates back at least to the eighteenth and nineteenth centuries when the belief among doctors and the general public was that a "constitutional weakness" ran in families and that this weakness produced alcoholics. With the growth of the temperance movement came an emphasis on the environmental causes and consequences of drinking. The issue of environment versus heredity now produces heated debate in the area of alcohol abuse. It is a complex issue, mostly addressed by studies of twins and adopted children, but few clear-cut findings are emerging. It seems safest to conclude that both factors play a role in the development of alcohol abuse and that the people most likely to become alcoholics have both a genetic and an environmental risk. However, another relevant question is "Why do the overwhelming majority of people who have both a genetic and an environmental risk never become alcoholics?" Nevertheless, a significant minority do, and we next need to consider why some people are more "vulnerable" than others.

Vulnerability and risk factors

It is likely that cognitive and behavioural disturbances may presage alcoholism (Tarter & Edwards, 1988). The findings implicating psychological disturbances are based on longitudinal investigations of children followed into adulthood who subsequently became alcohol-dependent, alcoholics' retrospective descriptions of their behaviour during childhood and adolescence, children at high risk for becoming alcoholic, twins discordant for drinking behaviour, and adolescents who present early signs of problem drinking. Much of this research effort has focused primarily on males.

In as much as alcoholism tends to run in families, the particular feature comprising the vulnerability may be more frequently or more strongly present in individuals with a family history of alcoholism.

Risk (for the development of alcohol abuse) has also been defined on the basis of sensation seeking, left-handedness, and Type A personality. Other vulnerability characteristics for substance abuse include poor school performance, perceived use of drugs by parents and other adults, psychological disorders (for example, depression and behaviour disturbance), low self-esteem, low religious involvement conflict with parents, lack of sense of purpose, a reduced sense of social responsibility, and childhood hyperactivity. However, each characteristic by itself is not a powerful predictor of outcome. Rather, it is typically the total number of factors that best predicts outcome.

It should be stressed that the presence of psychological features in childhood alone is not assumed to be sufficient to lead to an alcoholism outcome. This depends on a facilitating environment impacting on a person with a vulnerability to develop this condition: only a small proportion of these cases turn out to be "alcoholic".

Once the cognitive and behavioural characteristics of alcoholism vulnerability are more fully clarified, it will be feasible to implement targeted prevention procedures. For example, social skill disturbances, impulsivity, and anxiety symptoms are among the vulnerability traits that have been tentatively found to presage alcoholism. The rationale of such intervention strategies is that by improving the behaviours that presage alcoholism, the risk for developing this disorder is attenuated.

Can dissociation cause alcohol dependence?

State-dependent learning (SDL) or "dissociation" may be partially responsible for poor recall of events that take place during drinking (Lowe, 1988). This could, indeed, constitute the basis for "loss of control". After a few drinks, the alcoholic "forgets" the (negative) consequences of heavy drinking – consequences usually experienced in a relatively sober state.

The relevance of state-dependent learning to alcoholism also arises from the possibility of conditioned reactions to alcohol, as distinct from its unconditioned pharmacological effects. Alcoholics may drink to obtain access to behavioural or emotional repertoires that have become conditioned to the presence of alcohol, rather than to obtain any of the intrinsic effects of alcohol. Or intoxication may alter the user's sensitivity to social reinforcement so that reinforcing contingencies are effectively changed even in the absence of any real change in the external environment. Thus, in so far as the drinker has developed drug state behaviours that are more reinforcing than sober behaviours, the drug state will have acquired more positive aspects than it initially possessed, by virtue of its conditioned associations.

There is, incidentally, nothing about this argument that uniquely applies to alcoholism. It appears equally relevant to other substances with strong stimulus properties, such as nicotine, cannabis, and heroin (Overton, 1987).

CONCLUSION

Excessive and chronic alcohol ingestion would seem to be best viewed as a set of behaviours for which others might have been substituted, and intermittently are, rather than as a highly specific disorder or disease. Some aetiological, preventive, and therapeutic orientations emphasize the role of physical dependence and favour genetic influences as strong determinants of alcohol-related disorders. But many psychologists believe that severe dependence is the result of learning and conditioning. Psychological treatments are therefore being developed that reverse or modify this process. It is important to recognise that problem drinking is malleable, waxing and then entering periods of remission. Alcohol drinking, even in severely dependent individuals, remains susceptible to control by both antecedent and consequential environmental events.

DRUG ADDICTION

The human body is capable of tolerating and eliminating small quantities of virtually any substance or drug with no permanent or harmful effects. However, if large doses are ingested or if a drug is used frequently even though in small quantities, harmful effects on the person's physical or mental health may begin to appear. Generally, any use of a drug to a point where one's health is adversely affected or one's ability to function in society is impaired can be defined as *drug abuse*.

DEPENDENCE AND TOLERANCE

Physical dependence

The dangers of using a particular drug are often associated with the drug's potential to cause addiction, or physical dependence as it is commonly referred to. Many legal drugs, including barbiturates, tranquillizers, analgesics, opiates, alcohol, and tobacco, have this potential, and abusers can become physically dependent. Among the illegal drugs, only heroin leads to severe physical dependence, which means that complex physiological changes result from using the drug, so that *withdrawal symptoms* will occur if the addict abstains from using it. The withdrawal from a physically addicting drug invariably causes moderate to severe physical and mental symptoms.

The relationship between a withdrawal syndrome and drug dependence is complex. There are drugs which, if given repeatedly over a long period, produce physical dependence and therefore a withdrawal syndrome when they are discontinued. But for many of these drugs the syndrome is not necessarily accompanied by severe discomfort, anxiety, or even a marked desire to get more of the drug. So physical dependence need not equal "addiction" or "psychological dependence". A good example of this is the drug imipramine, which is used in the treatment of depression. When it is stopped after prolonged administration, there may be nausea, muscle aches, anxiety, and difficulty in sleeping but never a compulsion to resume the use of the drug (Jaffe, 1975).

Besides physical dependence, drugs can lead to habituation, and a second kind of physiological condition referred to as tolerance. Some people speak of "psychological" dependence, but this term has little scientific meaning beyond the notion that some activities, including drug taking, become part of one's habitual behaviour. Giving up the activity is accomplished only through much difficulty because the person has become habituated to it.

Habituation

Habituation is the repeated use of a drug because the user finds that each use increases pleasurable feelings or reduces feelings of anxiety, fear, or stress. Habituation becomes problematic when the person becomes so consumed by the need for the drug-altered state of consciousness that all of his or her energies are directed to compulsive drug-seeking behaviour. Physically addicting drugs such as heroin and alcohol typically produce habituation as well, so that the person is trapped into using all of his or her energies and resources for obtaining the drug. As a consequence of this compulsive drug-seeking behaviour, relationships, jobs, and families can be destroyed. Many of the widely used recreational drugs, including cannabis (marijuana), cocaine, LSD (lysergic acid diethylamide), PCP (phencyclidine, commonly called "angel dust"), and MDMA (methylenedioxymethamphetamine, also known as "Ecstasy") do *not* create physical dependence, but people do become habituated to their use. There are no physical symptoms of withdrawal from stopping use of these drugs, but people may experience uncomfortable psychological symptoms because of the habituation.

Tolerance

Drug tolerance is an adaptation of the body to a drug such that ever larger doses are needed to gain the same effect. The more tolerance potential a drug has, the more potentially dangerous it is. Because not all regions of the body become tolerant to the same degree, these higher doses may cause harmful side-effects to some parts of the body. For example, a heroin or barbiturate user can become tolerant to the psychological effects of the drug, but the brain's respiratory centre, which controls breathing, does not. If the dose of heroin, barbiturate, or other depressant becomes high enough, the brain's respiratory centre ceases to function and the person stops breathing.

There is a physiological component in dependence. It is usually called neurological adaptation, the state in which the brain adapts to the presence of alcohol (or other drugs). This state results in tolerance and also withdrawal symptoms when blood-drug levels decline. It is important to emphasize that neurological adaptation does not always lead to psychological dependence or habituation. For this reason the term *neuro-adaptation* is preferable to the term physical dependence. Neurological adaptation can be conditioned so that it is aroused by signals or associated stimuli in the absence of drugs. This leads to *behavioural tolerance* and conditioned withdrawal (Corfield-Sumner & Stolerman, 1978).

Siegel (1988) has demonstrated that tolerance to a drug's effect can best be understood in terms of an *anticipatory response* to this effect. Compensatory classically conditioned adaptive responses oppose a drug's action and these can be triggered by any cue that enables the individual to anticipate that the drug is imminent: that is, with a drug that the person has previously experienced. These responses may be triggered by environmental as well as internal stimuli.

Tolerance and dependence are independent properties. It is possible for a drug to produce tolerance but no dependence, and it is also possible that dependence can develop to a drug that has little or no tolerance potential. In addition, some drugs have both a tolerance and a dependency potential. Moreover, tolerance and dependence are not inevitable consequences of taking drugs. Not everyone who drinks alcohol, for instance, does so with sufficient frequency and in sufficient quantity to develop a tolerance, and most drinkers do not become dependent.

COMMONALITIES ACROSS ADDICTIVE BEHAVIOUR

"Addiction" is a complex, progressive behaviour pattern having biological, psychological, sociological, and behavioural components. What sets this behaviour pattern apart from others is the individual's overwhelmingly pathological involvement in or attachment to it, subjective compulsion to continue it, and reduced ability to exert personal control over it.

A distinction can be made between the "object of addiction" and the "addictive process" (Peele, 1985). The compulsive involvement in a behaviour pattern represents the addictive process. It is this process, along with its multidimensional determinants, that is comparable across different drugs of addiction (Lang, 1983).

The possibility that addiction to different drugs involves a common mechanism has considerable appeal. There is no presumption that addictions to all classes of drugs are identical: there are obvious differences among addictions to different drugs, and even individual cases involving the same drug can display marked differences. However, certain elements of addiction seem to be shared across distinctively different drugs and behaviour, and these similarities provide the impetus for developing unifying theories of addiction (Orford, 1985).

First, the addictive experience provides a potent and rapid means of changing one's mood and sensations because of both direct physiological effects and learned expectations (Peele, 1985). The individual engages in a form of self-indulgence for short-term pleasure or satisfaction, despite an awareness of the long-term negative consequences (Miller, 1980).

A second, and related, feature is that various physical and psychological states such as general arousal, stress, pain, or negative moods tend to be associated with and to influence the likelihood of engaging in the addictive behaviour. Alcohol and drug abusers typically use such substances co-occurrently or interchangeably (Istvan & Matarazzo, 1984). Moreover, coming off one substance often results in the abuse of another. In particular, alcohol and the benzodiazepines (minor tranquillizers) have been linked in this regard.

A third feature is the role of both classical and instrumental conditioning in the addictive process. The changes that are induced when the individual engages in the addictive behaviour serve as an unconditioned stimulus. Through repeated association with these changes, a wide variety of other stimuli acquire the power of conditioned stimuli. The latter may include mood states, cognitive expectations, and levels of physiological arousal, as well as more specific features of the social and physical environment in which the behaviour typically occurs. The presence of such conditioned stimuli may elicit changes that the individual interprets as a strong desire or craving for the addictive experience, and may also contribute to the contextual events that predict engaging in that behaviour.

Another commonality across addictions is the high rate of *relapse* following a period of abstinence (Marlatt & Gordon, 1985). It appears that a number of cognitive-expectational, emotional, and behavioural factors make comparable contributions to the relapse process in drinking, smoking, and drug use (Gossop, 1989).

Common "high risk" situations include negative emotional states such as anxiety, depression, boredom, and loneliness; interpersonal conflicts typically resulting in feelings of frustration, anger, and resentment; and social pressure associated with being in a physical, social or emotional context in which substance use has occurred in the past and is being directly encouraged by peers (Marlatt & Gordon, 1985).

An additional risk of relapse is the possibility of "triggering" a return to the target substance by engaging in alternative behaviour strongly linked with the target behaviour (Miller, 1980). This risk is high among multi-drug users.

Different functions

Although there are many who advocate a general mechanism underlying addiction to different drugs, others do not subscribe to this unitary theory. An extreme variation of the opposing multiple theory approach might assert that the cause of addiction to even a single drug varies with each individual. So we would need unique explanations for every case of addiction.

Psychopharmacologists have also shown that (potentially) addictive drugs may serve a number of different functions. And if the social context is taken into account, the list of such functions becomes potentially varied and vast.

For instance, in the smoking research area, Warburton (1988) suggests that the psychological effects of nicotine are much more subtle than those of other drugs, such as alcohol or heroin. He reviews evidence indicating that the psychological effects of nicotine are crucial to the maintenance of the smoking habit. He also suggests that the mechanisms by which the drug achieves this effect are quite different from those underlying other habitual substance use.

THEORETICAL APPROACHES

The field of addictive behaviour has previously been dominated by contributions from disciplines other than psychology – particularly from medicine and the neurosciences. A glut of popular and non-expert books has also appeared on the topic of addiction, many written by individuals who are themselves recovering from addictions. The frequent discrepancies between the approaches have added fuel to ongoing debates and have contributed to the divisive nature of the field.

Since the early 1970s there have been numerous publications in the biomedical and social sciences. Because of a parallel improvement in methodology, this research has produced a wealth of empirical data and theoretical insights. There has been a gradually growing conviction that the causes of dependency cannot be found within the limits of one single discipline. The various scientific search routes for explanations can be taken without interfering with one another, and each can contribute to unravelling the complexity of addictive behaviours. It is now generally agreed that addictive behaviours are multiply determined phenomena, and should be considered as biopsychosocial entities.

The biopsychosocial model

A major development in the addictions field since the early 1980s has been a move away from reductionist thinking and towards more integrative theories. Addiction is seen as being determined by the interaction of psychological, environmental, and physiological factors (Peele, 1985). This formulation is consistent with a biopsychosocial approach to health and illness (Schwartz, 1982).

Thus, addiction is a total experience involving physiological changes in individuals (some of whom may be genetically and/or psychologically predisposed). These changes are interpreted and given meaning by the individual within the sociocultural context in which the addictive behaviour occurs (Zinberg, 1981).

Within the biopsychosocial perspective, psychologists focus on the behaviour of individuals. This is in contrast with biomedical orientations, which focus on biological deviances (including constitutional or genetic aspects). Sociologists and cultural anthropologists, on the other hand, search for social and cultural factors, such as norms and cultural beliefs. Epidemiologists examine the social and economic factors that influence the spreading of addictive behaviours in groups or nations. Until the 1970s the interest of psychology in the subject of addiction had been scarce. Since then, however, developments have been impressive (e.g., Sobell & Sobell, 1987). This applies to questions of causation, to treatment possibilities, as well as to the function of assessment (Blane & Leonard, 1987; Donovan & Marlatt, 1988; Hester & Miller, 1989).

THE "ADDICTIVE" PERSONALITY?

Many studies of the addictive personality have been carried out in trying to find characteristics typical of the addictive individual. But convincing evidence has eluded researchers. The idea that a unitary set of personality factors precedes and results in the development of addictive disorders has not been widely accepted in alcohol and drug treatment research and theory. Indeed, some researchers minimize any causal role for personality factors in substance use.

In general, addictive populations appear to differ from non-addictive populations in that they show more deviancy. But specific addictive subgroups hardly differ from each other.

DRUGS AS REINFORCERS

Since the mid-1960s, powerful procedures have been developed to analyse the behavioural aspects of drug dependence in animals. This analysis is based on conditioning principles widely used by experimental psychologists and behavioural pharmacologists. For the analysis of drug-seeking behaviour, conditions are arranged so that a behavioural response is followed by the administration of a drug. If the response increases in frequency, then the drug is defined as a positive reinforcer for that behaviour.

A drug seems to be the ultimate reinforcer in that it is often quick-acting. If delivered in a very quick and intense way (for example, inhaling tobacco smoke or injecting heroin) its effects are certain and predictable. It affects basic reward mechanisms in the brain. A wide variety of psychoactive drugs have been shown to serve as positive reinforcers in both rats and monkeys. In general, drugs that serve as positive reinforcers in animals are those that produce dependence in humans.

Developments based on this methodology have led to a description of drug addiction as an extreme case of compulsive drug use associated with strong motivational effects of the drug (Bozarth, 1990). The "addiction potential" of a drug is derived from its ability to activate brain mechanisms involved in the control of normal behaviour – to such an extent that it can disrupt the individual's normal motivational hierarchy. This effect has been termed *motivational toxicity*.

At some point in the drug-use cycle there is a shift in control from intraper-sonal and sociological to pharmacological factors in governing drug-taking behaviour. This is concomitant with a marked increase in the motivational strength of the drug and with a progression from casual to compulsive drug use and ultimately to drug addiction. This may occur quite rapidly for some drugs, such as heroin or free-base cocaine, and much more slowly for other drugs, such as alcohol.

CONCLUSION

Many feel that the incidence and prevalence of drug addictive behaviours are increasing and that these problems are affecting a broad spectrum of individuals. At the same time there is an increase in interdisciplinary approaches to investigating the addictions. Addictions are best viewed as behaviours developed and maintained by multiple sources: they are multiply determined and multidimensional in nature. The most useful explanatory models take into account biological, psychological, and social components. Within the psychological components, (social) learning theory and cognitive-behavioural approaches have been particularly effective. The emergence of a biopsychosocial model in the areas of health psychology and behavioural medicine is another landmark. As applied specifically to the area of alcohol and drug addiction, an interactive biopsychosocial model provides a bridge across the varying perspectives of different disciplines, ideologies, and paradigms.

FURTHER READING

Edwards, G., & Lader, M. (Eds) (1990). *The nature of drug dependence*. Oxford: Oxford University Press.

Galizio, M., & Maisto, S. A. (Eds) (1985). *Determinants of substance abuse: Biological, psychological, and environmental factors*. New York: Plenum.

Lowe, G. (1984). Alcohol and alcoholism. In D. J. Sanger & D. E. Blackman (Eds) *Aspects of psychopharmacology* (pp. 84–109). London: Methuen.

Marlatt, G. A., Baer, J. S., Donovan, D. M., & Kivlahan, D. R. (1988). Addictive behaviors: Aetiology and treatment. *Annual Review of Psychology, 39,* 223–252.

Miller, W. R., & Heather, N. (Eds) (1986). *Treating addictive behaviors: Processes of change*. New York: Plenum.

REFERENCES

Babor, T. F., & Lauerman, R. J. (1986). Classification and forms of inebriety: Historical antecedents of alcoholic typologies. In M. Galanter (Ed.) *Recent developments in alcoholism* (vol. 4, pp. 13–144). New York: Plenum.

Blake, H. T., & Leonard, K. E. (Eds) (1987). *Psychological theories of drinking and alcoholism*. New York: Guilford.

Bozarth, M. A. (1990). Drug addiction as a psychobiological process. In D. M. Warburton (Ed.) *Addiction controversies* (pp. 112–134). London: Harwood Academic.

Brown, S. A., Goldman, M. S., & Christiansen, B. A. (1985). Do alcohol expectancies mediate drinking patterns of adults? *Journal of Consulting and Clinical Psychology, 53,* 512–519.

Conger, J. (1956). Reinforcement theory and the dynamics of alcoholism. *Quarterly Journal of Studies on Alcohol, 17,* 296–305.

Corfield-Sumner, P. K., & Stolerman, I.P. (1978). Behavioral tolerance. In D. E. Blackman & D. J. Sanger (Eds) *Contemporary research in behavioral pharmacology* (pp. 391–448). New York: Plenum.

Critchlow, B. (1986). The powers of John Barleycorn. *American Psychologist, 41,* 751–764.

Donovan, D. M., & Marlatt, G. A. (Eds) (1988). *Assessment of addictive behaviors*. New York: Guilford.

Edwards, G. (1986). The alcohol dependence syndrome: A concept as stimulus to enquiry. *British Journal of Addiction, 81,* 71–84.

Goldman, M. S., Brown, S. A., & Christiansen, B. A. (1987). Expectancy theory: Thinking and drinking. In H. T. Blane & K. E. Leonard (Eds) *Psychological theories of drinking and alcoholism* (pp. 181–226). New York: Guilford.

Gossop, M. (1989). *Relapse and addictive behaviour*. London: Tavistock/Routledge.

Hester, R. K., & Miller, W. R. (1989). *Handbook of alcoholism treatment approaches*. New York: Pergamon.

Hodgson, R. J. (1990). Cognitions and desire. In D. M. Warburton (Ed.) *Addiction controversies* (pp. 223–235). London: Harwood Academic.

Hull, J. G. (1981). A self-awareness model of the causes and effects of alcohol and consumption. *Journal of Abnormal Psychology, 90*, 586–600.

Istvan, J., & Matarazzo, J. D. (1984). Tobacco, alcohol, and caffeine use: A review of their interrelationships. *Psychological Bulletin, 95*, 301–326.

Jaffe, J. H. (1975) Drug addiction and drug abuse. In L. S. Goodman & A. Gilman (Eds) *The pharmacological basis of therapeutics* (pp. 284–324). New York: Macmillan.

Jellinek, E. M. (1960). *The disease concept of alcoholism*. New Brunswick, NJ: Hillhouse.

Lang, A. (1983). Addictive personality: A viable construct? In P. Levinson, D. Gerstein, & R. Maloff (Eds) *Commonalities in substance use and habitual behavior* (pp. 157–236). Lexington, MA: Lexington Books.

Lowe, G. (1981). State-dependent recall decrements with moderate doses of alcohol. *Current Psychological Research, 1*, 3–8.

Lowe, G. (1988). State-dependent retrieval effects with social drugs. *British Journal of Addiction, 83*, 99–103.

Lowe, G. (1990). Alcohol: A positive enhancer of pleasurable expectancies? In D. M. Warburton (Ed.) *Addiction controversies* (pp. 53–65). London: Harwood Academic.

Marlatt, G. A., & Donovan, D. M. (1982). Behavioral psychology approaches to alcoholism. In E. M. Pattison & E. Kaufman (Eds) *Encyclopaedic handbook of alcoholism* (pp. 560–576). New York: Gardner.

Marlatt, G. A., & Gordon, J. R. (Eds) (1985). *Relapse prevention: Maintenance strategies in addictive behavior change*. New York: Guilford.

Miller, W. R. (Ed.) (1980). *The addictive behaviors*. New York: Pergamon.

Moskowitz, H. (1979). The effects of alcohol and other drugs on skills performance and information processing. In G. Olive (Ed.) *Drug-action modifications: Comparative pharmacology. Advances in Pharmacology and Therapeutics, 8*, 211–221.

Orford, J. (1985). *Excessive appetites: A psychological view of addictions*. New York: Wiley.

Overton, D. A. (1987). Applications and limitations of the drug discrimination method for the study of drug abuse. In M. A. Bozarth (Ed.) *Methods of assessing the reinforcing properties of abused drugs* (pp. 291–340). Heidelberg: Springer-Verlag.

Peele, S. (1985). *The meaning of addiction: compulsive experience and its interpretation*. Lexington, MA: Lexington Books.

Rohsenow, D. J. (1982). Social anxiety, daily moods, and alcohol use over time among heavy social drinking men. *Addictive Behaviors, 7*, 311–315.

Schwartz, G. E. (1982). Testing the biopsychosocial model: The ultimate challenge facing behavioral medicine. *Journal of Consulting and Clinical Psychology, 50*, 1040–1053.

Sher, K. E., & Levenson, R. W. (1982). Risk for alcoholism and individual differences in the stress-response-dampening effect of alcohol. *Journal of Abnormal Psychology, 91*, 350–367.

Siegel, S. (1988). Drug anticipation and drug tolerance. In M. H. Lader (Ed.) *The psychopharmacology of addiction* (pp. 73–96). Oxford: Oxford University Press.

Sobell, L. C., & Sobell, M. B. (Eds) (1987). Two decades of behavioral research in the alcohol field: Change, challenge, and controversy (special issue). *Advances in Behavioral Research and Therapy, 9*, 59–72.

Tarter, R. E., & Edwards, K. (1988). Psychological factors associated with the risk for alcoholism. *Alcoholism: Clinical and Experimental Research, 12*, 471–480.

Warburton, D. M. (1988). The puzzle of nicotine use. In M. Lader (Ed.) *The psychopharmacology of addiction* (pp. 27–49). Oxford: Oxford University Press.

Zinberg, N. E. (1981). Social interactions, drug use, and drug research. In J. H. Lowinson & P. Ruiz (Eds) *Substance abuse: Clinical problems and perspectives.* Baltimore, MD: Williams & Wilkins.

GLOSSARY

This glossary is confined to a selection of frequently used terms that merit explanation or comment. Its informal definitions are intended as practical guides to meanings and usages. The entries are arranged alphabetically, word by word, and numerals are positioned as though they were spelled out.

abnormal psychology a branch of psychology, sometimes called psychopathology, concerned with the classification, aetiology (causation), diagnosis, treatment, and prevention of mental disorders (q.v.) and disabilities. *Cf.* clinical psychology.

acetylcholine one of the neurotransmitter (q.v.) substances that play a part in relaying information between neurons.

ACh a common abbreviation for acetylcholine (q.v.).

ACTH *see* adrenocorticotropic hormone (ACTH).

adrenal glands from the Latin *ad*, to, *renes*, kidneys, a pair of endocrine glands (q.v.), situated just above the kidneys, which secrete adrenalin (epinephrine), noradrenalin (norepinephrine) (qq.v.), and other hormones into the bloodstream. *See also* adrenocorticotropic hormone (ACTH).

adrenalin(e) hormone secreted by the adrenal glands (q.v.), causing an increase in blood pressure, release of sugar by the liver, and several other physiological reactions to perceived threat or danger. *See also* antidepressant drugs, endocrine glands, noradrenalin(e).

adrenocorticotropic hormone (ACTH) a hormone secreted by the pituitary gland that stimulates the adrenal gland (q.v.) to secrete corticosteroid hormones such as cortisol (hydrocortisone) into the bloodstream, especially in response to stress or injury.

affect any subjectively experienced feeling state or emotion, such as euphoria, anger, or sadness.

affective disorders an alternative term for mood disorders (q.v.).

afferent neurons from the Latin *ad*, to, *ferre*, to carry, neurons that transmit impulses from the sense organs to the central nervous system (CNS) (q.v.). *Cf.* efferent neurons.

agoraphobia from the Greek *agora*, market-place, *phobia*, fear, an irrational and debilitating fear of open places and of travelling or leaving home unaccompanied, often associated with panic attacks; one of the most common phobias (q.v.) encountered in clinical practice.

Alzheimer's disease named after the German physician who first identified it, a degenerative form of presenile dementia (q.v.), usually becoming manifest between the ages of 40 and 60, characterized by loss of memory and impairments of thought and speech. *See also* senile dementia.

amnesia partial or complete loss of memory. Anterograde amnesia is loss of memory for events following the amnesia-causing trauma, or loss of the ability to form long-term memories for new facts and events; retrograde amnesia is loss of memory for events occurring shortly before the trauma.

amphetamine any of a class of commonly abused drugs including Benzedrine, Dexedrine, and Methedrine that act as central nervous system stimulants, suppress appetite, increase heart-rate and blood pressure, and induce euphoria.

anorexia nervosa from the Greek *an*, lacking, *orexis*, appetite, an eating disorder, mostly of women, characterized by self-induced weight loss, a morbid fear of fatness which does not diminish as weight decreases, and a disturbance of body image (feeling fat even when emaciated). *Cf.* bulimia nervosa.

anterograde amnesia *see under* amnesia.

anti-anxiety drugs an umbrella term for a number of drugs, including the benzodiazepine drugs (q.v.) and the muscle relaxant meprobamate, that are used for reducing anxiety, also sometimes called minor tranquillizers.

antidepressant drugs drugs that influence neurotransmitters (q.v.) in the brain, used in the treatment of mood disorders (q.v.), especially depression (q.v.). The monoamine oxidase inhibitor (MAOI) drugs block the absorption of amines such as dopamine, adrenalin, and noradrenalin (qq.v.), allowing these stimulants to accumulate at the synapses in the brain, the tricyclic antidepressants such as imipramine act by blocking the re-uptake of noradrenalin in particular, thereby similarly increasing its availability, and the selective serotonin re-uptake inhibitor fluoxetine hydrochloride (Prozac) blocks the re-uptake of serotonin (q.v.).

antipsychotic drugs a general terms for all drugs used to alleviate the symptoms of psychotic disorders (q.v.). Major tranquillizers, including especially the phenothiazine derivatives such as chlorpromazine (Largactil) and thioridazine, are used primarily in the treatment of schizophrenia (q.v.) and other disorders involving psychotic symptoms; lithium compounds are used primarily in the treatnnent of bipolar (manic-depressive) disorder (q.v.). *See also* tardive dyskinesia.

anxiety disorders a group of mental disorders (q.v.) in which anxiety is an important symptom. *See also* obsessive-compulsive disorder, panic disorder, phobia, post-traumatic stress disorder (PTSD).

anxiolytic drugs another name for anti-anxiety drugs (q v.).

applied behaviour analysis the application of learning theory to behavioural problems in everyday settings, including hospitals, clinics, schools, and factories. Research and practice in this field is described by its practitioners as applied, behavioural, analytic, technological, conceptually systematic, effective, and capable of generalized effects. *See also* behaviour modification.

autistic disorder a severe mental disorder, with onset prior to 3 years of age, characterized by impaired social interaction, including abnormalities in eye contact and other non-verbal behaviours, failure to relate normally to peers and to share experiences with others, lack of emotional responsiveness, restricted, repetitive, and stereotyped behaviour patterns, and often delayed or absent language development, impaired ability to communicate verbally, or stereotyped and repetitive speech habits.

autonomic nervous system a subdivision of the nervous system (q.v.) that regulates (autonomously) the internal organs and glands. It is divided into the sympathetic nervous system and the parasympathetic nervous system (qq.v.).

barbiturates chemical compounds derived from barbituric acid, including barbitone and phenobarbitone, used as hypnotic or sedative drugs, liable to cause strong dependence when abused.

behaviour modification the application of techniques of operant conditioning (q.v.)

to reduce or eliminate maladaptive or problematic behaviour patterns or to develop new ones. *See also* applied behaviour analysis, cognitive-behaviour therapy, flooding.

behaviour therapy a therapeutic technique based on the principles of conditioning and behaviour modification (q.v.).

benzodiazepine drugs any of a group of chemical compounds that are used as anti-anxiety drugs (q.v.) and hypnotics (sleeping drugs), including diazepam (Valium) and chlordiazepoxide (Librium).

bipolar disorder a mood disorder (q.v.) in which depression alternates with mania, also known as manic-depressive psychosis.

blood-brain barrier a complex physiological mechanism whose function is to allow blood to flow freely to the brain but to prevent some chemicals present in the blood from reaching the brain.

borderline personality disorder a mental disorder (q.v.) in which a person hovers on the borderline between normal and disordered functioning, typically with disturbed social relations, dramatic mood swings, and often outbursts of anger and impulsive episodes of antisocial behaviour.

bulimia nervosa from the Greek *bous*, ox, *limos*, hunger, an eating disorder, confined almost exclusively to women, characterized by recurrent episodes of binge eating, usually followed by self-induced vomiting and/or laxative abuse, and a morbid fear of fatness. *Cf.* anorexia nervosa.

catecholamine any member of the group of hormones (q.v.) that are catechol derivatives, especially adrenalin, noradrenalin, and dopamine, (qq.v.), all of which are involved in the functioning of the nervous system (q.v.).

central limit theorem in statistics, a theorem showing (roughly) that the sum of any large number of unrelated variables tends to be distributed according to the normal distribution (q.v.). It explains why psychological and biological variables that are due to the additive effects of numerous independently acting causes are distributed approximately normally.

central nervous system (CNS) in human beings and other vertebrates, the brain and spinal cord.

chlordiazepoxide one of the benzodiazepine drugs (q.v.), commonly called Librium.

clinical psychology one of the major professions of psychology, concerned with the prevention, diagnosis, treatment, and study of mental disorders (q.v.) and disabilities, to be distinguished from abnormal psychology (q.v.), which is the academic study of these matters.

CNS *see* central nervous system (CNS).

cognitive-behaviour therapy techniques of psychotherapy based on methods of behaviour modification (q.v.) with an emphasis on the learning of cognitive responses involving imagery, fantasy, thoughts, and above all beliefs.

compulsions repetitive, ritualised, stereotyped actions, such as hand-washing, that a person feels unable to stop performing in spite of realizing that the behaviour is inappropriate or excessive, often associated with obsessions (q.v.).

correlation in statistics, the relationship between two variables such that high scores on one tend to go with high scores on the other or (in the case of negative correlation) such that high scores on one tend to go with low scores on the other. The usual index of correlation, called the product-moment correlation coefficient and symbolized by r, ranges from 1.00 for perfect positive correlation, through zero for uncorrelated variables, to -1.00 for perfect negative correlation.

correlational study a non-experimental type of research design in which patterns of correlations (q.v.) are analysed.

97

DA a common abbreviation for dopamine (q.v.).

delusion a false personal belief, maintained in the face of overwhelming contradictory evidence, excluding religious beliefs that are widely accepted by members of the person's culture or sub-culture, characteristic especially of delusional (paranoid) disorder (q.v.). *Cf.* hallucination.

delusional (paranoid) disorder formerly called paranoia, a mental disorder characterized by delusions (q.v.), especially of jealousy, grandeur, or persecution, but with otherwise unimpaired intellectual functioning.

dementia from the Latin *de* away from, *mens*, mind, any mental disorder characterized by a failure or loss of mental powers, especially memory, intelligence, and orientation. *See also* Alzheimer's disease, dementia praecox, presenile dementia, senile dementia.

dementia praecox from the Latin for dementia of youth (as opposed to senile dementia), an obsolete term for schizophrenia (q.v.).

deoxyribonucleic acid (DNA) a self-replicating molecule, the major constituent of chromosomes, containing the hereditary information transmitted from parents to offspring in all organisms apart from some viruses (including the AIDS virus), and consisting of two strands coiled into a double helix linked by hydrogen bonds between the complementary chemical bases that encode the genetic information – between adenine and thymine and between cytosine and guanine. *See also* gene.

depersonalization a form of dissociation (q.v.) involving a feeling of loss of the sense of self, sometimes accompanied by an out-of-body experience (OBE) – a sense of perceiving oneself from a distance, usually from above – associated with sleep deprivation, some forms of drug intoxication, and various mental disorders including some forms of schizophrenia and dissociative disorder (qq.v.).

depression a sustained negative mood state characterized by sadness, pessimism, a general feeling of despondency, passivity, indecisiveness, suicidal thoughts, sleep disturbances, and other mental and physical symptoms, associated with some mood disorders (q.v.).

desensitization, systematic a technique of behaviour therapy or behaviour modification (qq.v.) used for eliminating phobias (q.v.) in which the individual is exposed to a graded hierarchy of anxiety-eliciting stimuli under conditions of deep relaxation until the most frightening item can be confronted without tension.

diazepam one of the benzodiazepine drugs (q.v.), commonly called Valium.

dissociation a process involving a group of psychological functions having a degree of unity among themselves which become detached from the rest of personality and function more or less independently, as in multiple personality disorder (q.v.).

dissociative disorder an umbrella term for psychological disorders, such as multiple personality disorder and the non-organic amnesias, involving dissociation (q.v.) and general disintegration of the functions of consciousness, self-concept, or perceptual-motor coordination.

DNA *see* deoxyribonucleic acid (DNA).

dopamine a catecholamine (q.v.); one of the neurotransmitter (q.v.) substances significantly involved in central nervous system functioning. *See also* antidepressant drugs.

DSM-IV the common name of the fourth edition of the *Diagnostic and Statistical Manual of Mental Disorders* of the American Psychiatric Association, published in 1994, replacing DSM-III-R, the revised version of the third edition published in 1987, containing the most authoritative classification and definitions of mental disorders (q.v.).

ECT *see* electroconvulsive therapy (ECT).

efferent neurons from the Latin *e*, from, *ferre*, to carry, neurons that transmit impulses away from the central nervous system (CNS) towards the muscles, glands, etc. *Cf.* afferent neurons.

electroconvulsive therapy (ECT) a psychiatric method of treating certain symptoms of mental disorder by passing a weak electric current (20–30 milliamps) through the brain to induce *grand mal* epileptic-type convulsions in patients who are usually first given sedative and muscle relaxant drugs. Sometimes called shock therapy or electroshock therapy (EST).

endocrine gland any ductless gland, such as the adrenal gland or pituitary gland (qq.v.), that secretes hormones (q.v.) directly into the bloodstream. The endocrine system functions as an elaborate signalling system within the body, alongside the nervous system.

endorphins from the Greek *endon*, within, and morphine, from *Morpheus*, the Greek god of sleep and dreams, any of a class of morphine-like substances occurring naturally in the brain that bind to pain receptors and thus block pain sensations.

epinephrine, norepinephrine from the Greek *epi*, upon, *nephros*, kidney, alternative words for adrenalin and noradrenalin (qq.v.), especially in United States usage. *See also* endocrine gland.

fight or flight mechanism a response to perceived danger or threat in which catecholamines (q.v.) are released into the bloodstream and physiological arousal increases, temporarily increasing the organism's chances of survival, either by staying and fighting or fleeing.

5-hydroxytryptamine (5-HT) another name for serotonin (q.v.).

flooding a technique of behaviour therapy (q.v.) for treating phobias (q.v.) in which the client is exposed to the phobic stimulus for extended periods of time without the opportunity of escape.

fluoxetine hydrochloride *see under* antidepressant drugs.

gene from the Greek *genes*, born, the unit of hereditary transmission encoded in deoxyribonucleic acid (DNA) (q.v.), occupying a fixed locus on a chromosome, and either specifying the formation of a protein or part of a protein (structural gene) or regulating or repressing the operation of other genes (operator or repressor gene). The complete human genome contains between 50,000 and 100,000 genes.

hallucination from the Latin *alucinari*, to wander in the mind, a false perception, most commonly visual or auditory, subjectively similar or identical to an ordinary perception but occurring in the absence of relevant sensory stimuli, characteristic in particular of some forms of schizophrenia (q.v.). False perceptions occurring during sleep, while falling asleep (hypnagogic image), or while awakening (hypnopompic image) are not normally considered to be hallucinations. *Cf.* delusion.

hallucinogenic drugs drugs such as lysergic acid diethylamide (LSD) or mescaline that induce hallucinations.

homeostasis from the Greek *homos*, same, *stasis*, stoppage, the maintenance of equilibrium in any physiological or psychological process by automatic compensation for disrupting changes.

hormone from the Greek *horman*, to stir up or urge on, a chemical substance secreted into the bloodstream by an endocrine gland (q.v.) and transported to another part of the body where it exerts a specific effect.

hypnotics barbiturates and benzodiazepine drugs (qq.v.) used as sleeping drugs to treat insomnia and known informally as sleeping drugs.

imipramine *see under* antidepressant drugs.

intelligence from the Latin *intelligere*, to understand, the ability to think, in itself not directly observable, but manifested in such examples of intelligent behaviour as reasoning and problem solving, and measurable by intelligence quotient (IQ) (q.v.) tests.

intelligence quotient (IQ) a term introduced by the German psychologist William Stern in 1912 to denote a person's mental age divided by his or her chronological (actual) age. It became customary to multiply this quotient by 100 in order to express mental age as a percentage of chronological age, but in contemporary psychometric practice IQ scores are defined statistically without reference to the ratio of mental to chronological age: a person's IQ is defined by reference to a hypothetical population of IQ scores in a normal distribution (q.v.) with a mean (average) of 100 and a standard deviation (q.v.) of 15.

IQ *see under* intelligence quotient.

Largactil the trademark of a preparation of one of the antipsychotic drugs (q.v.), chlorpromazine.

Librium the trademark of a preparation of the drug chlordiazepoxide (q.v.). *See also* benzodiazepine drugs.

limbic system a ring of structures surrounding the brain stem concerned with emotion, hunger, and sex.

lithium *see under* antipsychotic drugs.

major tranquillizers *see under* antipsychotic drugs.

mania a mood disorder characterized by extreme elation, expansiveness, irritability, talkativeness, inflated self-esteem, and flight of ideas.

manic-depressive psychosis *see* bipolar disorder.

MAO inhibitor *see under* antidepressant drugs.

mental disorder according to DSM-IV (q.v.), a psychological or behavioural syndrome or pattern associated with distress (a painful symptom), disability (impairment in one or more areas of functioning), and a significantly increased risk of death, pain, disability, or an important loss of freedom, occurring not merely as a predictable response to a disturbing life-event.

minor tranquillizers another name for anti-anxiety drugs (q.v.).

monoamine oxidase inhibitor (MAOI) *see under* antidepressant drugs.

mood disorders a group of mental disorders characterized by disturbances of affect or mood, including especially depression, bipolar disorder and mania (qq.v.).

multiple personality disorder a rare dissociative disorder (q.v.) in which two or more markedly different personalities coexist within the same individual, popularly confused with schizophrenia (q.v.).

nervous system *see under* autonomic nervous system, central nervous system (CNS), parasympathetic nervous system, sympathetic nervous system.

neurophysiology the study of the operation of the nervous system (q.v.).

neurosis an obsolescent umbrella term for a group of mental disorders (q.v.) that are distressing but do not involve gross impairment of psychological functioning or any loss of self-insight or contact with reality. *See* anxiety disorders, obsessive-compulsive disorder, panic disorder, phobia, post-traumatic stress disorder (PTSD).

neurotransmitter a chemical substance such as acetylcholine, dopamine, serotonin, or noradrenalin (qq.v.) by which a neuron (nerve cell) communicates with another neuron or with a muscle or gland.

noradrenalin one of the catecholamine (q.v.) hormones and an important neurotransmitter (q.v.) in the nervous system, also called norepinephrine, especially in United States usage.

norepinephrine *see* noradrenalin.

normal distribution a symmetrical, bell-shaped probability distribution, with the most probable scores concentrated around the mean (average) and progressively less probable scores occurring further from the mean: 68.26 per cent of scores fall within one standard deviation (q.v.) on either side of the mean, 95.44 per cent fall within two standard deviations, and 99.75 fall within three standard deviations. Because of the central limit theorem (q.v.), the normal distribution approximates the observed frequency distributions of many psychological and biological variables and is widely used in inferential statistics.

obsessions recurrent, persistent, irrational ideas, thoughts, images, or impulses that are experienced not as voluntary but as unwanted invasions of consciousness, characteristic especially of obsessive-compulsive disorder (q.v.).

obsessive-compulsive disorder one of the more common anxiety disorders characterized, as the name suggests, by obsessions and compulsions (qq.v.)

operant conditioning a type of learning, sometimes called instrumental conditioning, which focuses on the process by which behaviour changes as a result of its consequences, in particular the way in which an individual's behavioural responses become more or less frequent as a consequence of reinforcement (q.v.).

panic disorder an anxiety disorder characterized by panic attacks, overwhelming apprehension, dread or terror, fear of going insane or dying, and fight or flight behaviour.

paranoia *see* delusional (paranoid) disorder.

parasympathetic nervous system one of the two major divisions of the autonomic nervous system; its general function is to conserve metabolic energy. *Cf.* sympathetic nervous system.

peptides chemical substances such as endorphins (q.v.) that regulate various bodily functions and play an important part in the experience of pain.

personality disorder any of a group of mental disorders (q.v.) characterized by deeply ingrained, enduring, maladaptive patterns of behaviour that cause suffering to the person with the disorder or to others.

phobia from the Greek *phobos*, fear, an irrational, debilitating, persistent, and intense fear of a specific type of object, activity, or situation, which, if certain diagnostic criteria are fulfilled, may be considered a mental disorder. *See also* agoraphobia.

pituitary gland the master endocrine gland (q.v.), attached by a stalk to the base of the brain, which secretes into the bloodstream hormones affecting bodily growth and the functioning of other endocrine glands. *See also* adrenocorticotropic hormone (ACTH).

post-traumatic stress disorder (PTSD) an anxiety disorder resulting from experience of a major traumatic event, characterized by obsessive reliving of the trauma in fantasies and dreams, a feeling of emotional numbness and lack of engagement in the world, sleep disturbances, an exaggerated startle response, general symptoms of anxiety, and in some cases (e.g. survivors of concentration camps) guilt about having survived.

presenile dementia a form of dementia (q.v.) of unknown cause starting before old age. *See also* Alzheimer's disease.

Prozac the proprietary name for fluoxetine hydrochloride, one of the antidepressant drugs (q.v.).

psychoactive drug any drug such as lysergic acid diethylamide (LSD), opium, or a barbiturate, that is capable of affecting mental activity. *See also* amphetamine, anti-anxiety drugs, antidepressant drugs, antipsychotic drugs, barbiturates, benzodiazepine drugs, hallucinogenic drugs, psychopharmacology.

psychology from the Greek *psyche*, mind, *logos*, study, the study of the nature, functions, and phenomena of behaviour and mental experience.

psychopathology *see* abnormal psychology.

psychopharmacology the study of drugs that have psychological effects. *See also* amphetamine, anti-anxiety drugs, antidepressant drugs, antipsychotic drugs, barbiturates, benzodiazepine drugs, hallucinogenic drugs, psychoactive drugs.

psychosis gross impairment of psychological functioning, including loss of self-insight and of contact with reality, such as is found in mental disorders involving hallucinations and delusions (qq.v.). *Cf.* neurosis.

receptor a sense organ or structure that is sensitive to a specific form of physical energy and that transmits neural information to other parts of the nervous system (q.v.).

reinforcement in learning theory, the strengthening of the bond between a stimulus and a response or anything that increases the relative frequency of a response.

reinforcer any stimulus or event that increases the relative frequency of a response during the process of reinforcement (q.v.).

schizophrenia from the Greek *schizein*, to split, *phren*, mind, a group of mental disorders characterized by incoherent thought and speech, hallucinations (q.v.), delusions (q.v.), flattened or inappropriate affect, deterioration of social functioning, and lack of self-care. In spite of its derivation, the word does not refer to multiple personality disorder (q.v.).

senile dementia from the Latin senilis, old, + dementia, dementia (q.v.) of unknown cause in old people, often associated with Alzheimer's disease (q.v.).

serotonin one of the neurotransmitter (q.v.) substances in the nervous system, also known as 5-hydroxytryptamine or 5-HT.

significance (statistical) a property of the results of an empirical investigation suggesting that they are unlikely to be due to chance factors alone. The 5 per cent level of significance has become conventional in psychology; this means that results are normally considered to be statistically significant if statistical tests show that the probability of obtaining results at least as extreme by chance alone is less than 5 per cent, usually written $p < .05$.

somatoform disorders a class of mental disorders (q.v.) characterized by deterioration of physical functioning without any discernable physiological cause, specifically when there is evidence that the physical symptoms have psychological causes and there is lack of voluntary control over the physical symptoms and indifference to the deterioration of physical functioning.

standard deviation a measure of dispersion or variability expressed in the same units as the scores themselves, equal to the square root of the variance (q.v.).

state-dependent memory memory for information learned in a particular state of consciousness – for example, in a particular emotional state or under the influence of alcohol or drugs – that can be recalled only when in a similar state. Thus material learned in an intoxicated state is sometimes remembered only in a later intoxicated state, and a person in a depressed state may be more likely to remember unhappy experiences from the past, which might exacerbate the depression and create a vicious circle.

stimulants hormones such as adrenalin, noradrenalin, and dopamine (qq.v.), and drugs such as amphetamines (q.v.), that increase physiological arousal in general and central nervous system activity in particular.

sympathetic nervous system one of the two major divisions of the autonomic nervous system; it is concerned with general activation, and it mobilizes the body's reaction to stress or perceived danger. *Cf.* parasympathetic nervous system.

systematic desensitization a technique of behaviour therapy (q.v.) pioneered by the South African psychiatrist Joseph Wolpe for treating phobias (q.v.) and specific anxieties, in which the client enters a state of deep muscle relaxation and is then exposed to a hierarchy of progressively more anxiety-arousing situations, real or imagined.

tardive dyskinesia from the Latin *tardus*, sluggish, and the Greek *dys*, bad, *kinesis*, movement, an irreversible neurological side-effect of over-use of antipsychotic drugs (q.v.), the symptoms of which include repetitive sucking, lip-smacking, and characteristic tongue movements.

tranquillizers *see under* anti-anxiety drugs, antipsychotic drugs.

tricyclic antidepressants *see* antidepressant drugs.

Valium a trademark of a preparation of the drug diazepam (q.v.). *See also* benzodiazepine drugs.

variability in statistics, the degree to which a set of scores is scattered. Thus two sets of scores with identical means (averages) may have widely different variabilities. The usual measures of variability are the variance and the standard deviation (qq.v.).

variance a measure of the dispersion or variability (q.v.) of a set of scores; it is equal to the mean (average) of the squared deviations of the scores from their mean. *See also* standard deviation.

INDEX

abnormal behaviour, definition ix–xi
addiction
    addictive behaviour 88–9
    addictive personality 90–1
    reinforcement 91
    theories of 80–3, 90
    see also alcohol; drugs
adrenaline, and anxiety 11
affective psychoses
    diagnosis 25–6
    and eating disorders 66–7
    features of 27, 30
    incidence 24
    treatment and prognosis 40
    see also manic-depressive psychosis
age
    and eating disorders 60, 61
    and schizophrenia 31
agoraphobia 14–15, 17
Agras, W.S. 71
alcohol, effects of 77–9
alcohol addiction xiii
    causes 79–83
    definition 79, 81
    treatment 83, 84
    vulnerability to 84
alcohol dependence syndrome 81–2
amenorrhoea 56, 57, 58, 64
Amenson, C.S. 4
Andreasen, N.C. 29
anorexia nervosa xii–xiii
    and affective disorder 66, 67
    beliefs and attitudes 63, 67–8
    causes 65–9
    diagnostic criteria 56–9
    eating habits 57–9, 61–2
    incidence 59–60
    neurotic symptoms 63
    personality predisposition 65

physical effects 64
    treatment and outcome 69–70, 71–2
anxiety
    and eating disorders 63
    nature and symptoms 11–13
    theories of 16–18
    treatment of 18–19, 20
    types of 13–16
attention
    cognitive bias and anxiety 13
    joint attention skills 45, 52–3
attributional distortion 8, 20
auditory hallucinations 28–9, 37
autism xii
    causes 46–7
    cognitive mechanisms 51–2
    diagnosis 45, 52–3
    language and social deficits 38, 45, 47–50
    mind-blindness theory 49–50
    nature and incidence 45–6
    treatment 53

barbiturates, tolerance 87
Baren-Cohen, S. 45, 49, 50, 51, 52, 53
behaviour
    abnormal ix–xi
    addictive 88–9
    repetitive 15–16, 45
behavioural models
    of addiction 80, 82–3, 88–9, 90
    of anxiety 16–17
behavioural therapy
    for anxiety 18–19
    for autism 53
    for schizophrenia 39
belief, autistic understanding of 49–50
Bettleheim, B. 47
biopsychosocial model of addiction 90